Polar Bears

Living with the White Bear

Nikita Ovsyanikov

Voyageur Press

Edited by Jane McHughen Publishing Services
Designed by Leslie Ross

Printed in Hong Kong

96 97 98 99 00 5 4 3 2 1

Library of Congress Cataloging-in-Publication Data
Ovsyanikov, Nikita.
Polar bears : living with the white bear / by Nikita Ovsyanikov.
p. cm.
Includes bibliographical references (p.142) and index.
ISBN 0-89658-277-9
1. Polar bear—Behavior.   I. Title.
QL737.C270925   1996
599.74'446—dc20   96-33764
CIP

Published by Voyageur Press, Inc.
123 North Second Street, P.O. Box 338, Stillwater, MN 55082 U.S.A.
612-430-2210, fax 612-430-2211

Please write or call, or stop by, for our free catalog of natural history publications. Our toll-free number to place an order or to obtain a free catalog is 800-888-WOLF (800-888-9653).

Educators, fundraisers, premium and gift buyers, publicists, and marketing managers: Looking for creative products and new sales ideas? Voyageur Press books are available at special discounts when purchased in quantities, and special editions can be created to your specifications. For details contact the marketing department.

Frontispiece: A young polar bear surveys its ice- and snow-covered domain on the coast of Wrangel Island, overlooking the East Siberian Sea.
Title pages: In January, the land of the polar bear—Wrangel and Herald Islands—is swathed in cold, and the sun does not shine for two full months. Arctic night starts here on November 22, and only on January 22 does the sun again appear above the horizon and then for just a brief period each day.
Opposite: Sitting on the edge of an ice floe on the coast of Wrangel Island, a mature male polar bear watches over the sea.

Contents

Dedication

To my mother, Galina Ovsyanikov. It is due to her love, patience, and understanding that I could spend so much time in the Arctic.

Acknowledgments

I greatly appreciate all of the support and assistance provided by the staff of the Nature Reserve at Wrangel Island during all of my four seasons of field work with polar bears on both Wrangel and Herald Islands.

My special thanks go to those people who were my companions in the field, sharing with me the wonderful time that I spent living with the white bears: my wife Irina Menushina, Jury Al'paun, Leonid Bove, Grisha Kaurgin, Anatoli Kochnev, Hugh Maynard, Igor Oleinikov, and Martin Saunders.

I thank Dan Guravich and Downs Matthews for joining us in spring 1992 in Camp Thomas on Wrangel and for their great interest in our experience. I also wish to thank Downs, now my good friend, for his kind editorial advice.

Nikita Ovsyanikov
Moscow
February 1996

A mother polar bear leads her two cubs in a charge to scare away an intruding male bear.

Prologue

Face to Face With the White Bear

I turned the all-terrain vehicle around the slope, drove up the coast toward the log cabin, and stopped in surprise—my way was blocked by at least six mature polar bears. They seemed agitated and scarcely acknowledged my presence, but still, they blocked my route. On the beach behind the cabin, walruses were barking. I edged the ATV forward and stopped, keeping the engine running. A huge male bear approached, sniffing the air.

I hesitated. The cabin was only eighty feet (25 m) from the beach, and I did not know whether the walruses were basking on the shore or swimming in the sea. I did not want to drive up to the cabin door for fear I might disturb the walruses if they were on the beach, but there was no way to reach the cabin on foot without getting mixed up with the polar bears. I was still hesitating when the bear took the initiative and walked toward me. His approach forced me to react, and I circled in front of him with the ATV. He stopped and regarded me for some time before getting worried and leaving the scene. The other bears scattered.

The way to the cabin was now clear, but I suspected it would not be long before the bears returned.

Darkness was falling fast, and I had no time to investigate what the bears who had greeted me were doing now that they had abandoned the cabin. Leaving the ATV, I walked to the cabin and looked out to the beach beyond. An amazing sight met my eyes: tens of thousands of walruses were churning up the sea. They were all in the water, which meant I could drive the ATV right up to the cabin without fear of disturbing them. Eager to unload before the bears drifted back, I rushed to the ATV and drove it up to the door. I hurried to get the food and equipment inside, and I parked the ATV in a shed near the cabin, hidden away from prying polar bear eyes.

My investigation into the life and behavior of polar bears in the Soviet Arctic had begun.

Face to face with a polar bear, Cape Blossom, Wrangel Island
Arriving at the observation cabin on Cape Blossom, I was greeted by a massive male polar bear blocking my route. The bear approached, seemingly without fear or hesitation, sniffing my scent on the air, obviously inquisitive about this human newcomer entering into his domain.

Introduction

At the Top of the World

If you scan the Arctic on a map of the world, you will see that there are only two significant land masses in the vast marine region north of Siberia and across to the Bering Strait: Wrangel and Herald Islands in the Chukchi Sea. The Bering Strait is a gate between the Arctic and Pacific Oceans, and the relatively shallow waters of the Chukchi Sea provide rich feeding grounds for the diversity of marine life in the area. This is the corner of the Arctic where I had chosen to study the largest non-aquatic carnivore in the world: the polar bear, *Ursus maritimus*.

The polar bear is a circumpolar species. In the Russian sector of the Arctic, three distinct populations have been identified. To the west is the Spitzbergen–Novaya Zemlya population, which is estimated at 4,200 to 5,700 animals. The smallest population, at 800 to 1,200 animals, is found around the Laptev Sea in the central Siberian sector of the Arctic Ocean. The third population inhabits the Chukchi Sea region and in the winter expands its range into the northern reaches of the Bering Strait. The territory covered by the bears in this population includes parts of eastern Siberia and western Alaska. Other populations of polar bears are found where food resources are rich enough to support them: the Beaufort Sea region of the Canadian Arctic archipelago and parts of Greenland. The southernmost population of polar bears in the world inhabits Hudson Bay in Canada.

Polar bears on the ice, Cape Blossom, Wrangel Island
Polar bears (*Ursus maritimus*) inhabit areas circumnavigating the North Pole from Siberia to Alaska, Canada to Greenland, with the southernmost population of the white bears inhabiting Hudson Bay in Canada. The white bears live on the Arctic ice as often as on land, and here a mother bear leads her two year-old cubs across the ice encasing the coast of Wrangel Island toward the open water of the Chukchi Sea in late autumn to search for food.

Pasqueflowers, Wrangel Island

Wrangel Island was not covered by ice during the last Ice Age and today remains a rare relic of the ancient tundra steppe, looking much as it did during the Pleistocene era of about one million years ago. Thus, the flora of Wrangel's steppe is rich in variety, considering how far north the island is situated: more than 380 species of plants are found on Wrangel, including this pasqueflower (*Pulsatilla nuttaliana*). The flora of Wrangel is richer in species than the whole of the Canadian Arctic archipelago, and the percentage of species particular to Wrangel is unusually high.

Wrangel Island is a unique part of our planet, untouched by glaciers during the last Ice Age and looking much as it would have done in the Pleistocene era, a true relic of the tundra steppe.

Polar bears range far and wide across the Arctic in search of food. In these vast expanses of open space, there are actually few areas where the food base is relatively stable and available year-round. In this respect, Wrangel Island is unique, making it one of the best places in the world to observe polar bears. The concentration of polar bear maternity dens is exceptionally high on both Wrangel and Herald Islands, and Herald boasts the highest concentration of polar bear dens in the entire Arctic region. On these islands I was to spend eight seasons living with the bears.

Not only as polar bear habitat, but in many other ecological respects, Wrangel Island is a unique part of our planet. The island was untouched by glaciers during the last Ice Age and looks much as it would have done in the Pleistocene era about one million years before the present day: It is a true relic of the tundra steppe. The flora on the island is extraordinarily rich for such a high latitude. More than 380 species of plants grow and blossom on Wrangel, covering the island in a fantastic carpet of color in the brief Arctic summer. More than 150 species of birds have been recorded on the island and 50 species are known to nest here. Besides polar bears, mammals on the island include Arctic foxes and two endemic species of lemmings. Introduced reindeer and musk-oxen thrive on the rich vegetation.

Winds blow over the island almost constantly and are especially severe in winter. Polar night when the sun does not rise above the horizon begins on November 22 and lasts until January 22. Snow covers the land for more than 240 days out of 365, and the temperature rises above 32 degrees Fahrenheit (0 degrees Celsius) for only two and a half months a year. The northern part of the island is dotted with shallow lakes that are covered with waterfowl in the summer and are frozen solid in the winter. In the center, running east and west to the coasts, several mountain ranges are separated from one another by wide river valleys. The highest mountain is 3,600 feet (1,091 m) above sea level.

Eight species of seabirds nest on Wrangel and Herald Islands. Their colonies cover the cliffs on the western and eastern shores of Wrangel and the complete 13.5-mile (22.5-km) coastline of Herald. A recent survey estimated that 140,000 seabirds nest on Herald, with twice as many on the cliffs of Wrangel. The presence of so many seabirds points to the abundance of fish and marine invertebrates on which the birds feed. The birds, in turn, enrich the surrounding waters with their excrement, providing food for phytoplankton, which are the basis for the food chain that builds from marine invertebrates to fish, seals, and, finally, polar bears.

Seals are the main prey for polar bears all over the Arctic, and two species of seals—the ringed seal, *Phoca hispida,* and the bearded seal, *Erignathus barbatus*—are plentiful around Wrangel. In the Wrangel Island region, where seal breeding dens are rarely found on flat ice because ice pressure around the islands forms numerous ice ridges, polar bears hunt seals at polynyas (areas of open water amid the sea ice)

Above: Wrangel Island

Known as Ostrov Vrangel'a in Anglicized Russian, Wrangel Island lies on the border between the Chukchi Sea and the East Siberian Sea north of the far northeastern region of Siberia. Well within the Arctic Circle and bisected by the 71° latitude, Wrangel is approximately parallel with Alaska's Point Barrow, the northernmost tip of the United States. It is also bisected by the 180° longitude, and thus portions of the island rest in both the Western and Eastern hemispheres.

Left: Snow geese, Wrangel Island

Snow geese (*Chen caerulescens*) are common on Wrangel Island, where they nest in large numbers. In former times, snow geese inhabited the Siberian north from Chukotka to Taimir, but have been almost exterminated by overhunting and reindeer herding. These colonies on Wrangel are the last remaining snow goose nesting areas in Asia. After the eggs hatch, the adult geese will lead their chicks to the northern region of Wrangel where they will settle at several lakes to molt.

"Black floe" of walruses, Wrangel Island
Walruses as well as seals are plentiful around Wrangel Island, and both are prey for polar bears. Many Pacific walruses (*Odobenus rosmarus divergens*) summer along the coasts of Wrangel, hauling out to rest and sun themselves on ice floes, which help to shield them from predators such as the white bears as well as humans on hunting ships. The Chukchi and Yupik Native people of Chukotka, the northeastern tip of Siberia, call ice floes covered by the resting walruses "black floes."

and leads (channels of open water), where seals come to breathe and haul out onto the edge of the ice to rest. Both Wrangel and Herald Islands act as ice breakers in the ocean: As the wind pushes the pack ice up against the islands, the ice is opened up into leads and open windows. Because of the numerous openings in the pack ice year-round, as long as there is ice, polar bears can hunt seals in the vicinity of the islands even in the coldest seasons.

Wrangel Island is also one of the key areas in the world for the Pacific walrus. For many years, thousands of walruses—about half the total population of this subspecies—have swum to Wrangel each spring to spend the summer in its coastal waters. Between 90 and 95 percent of the walruses that visit are females with young; about a third of the mothers are lactating and have calves younger than three years old. Most seasons, the male walruses spend their summers apart from the females and calves in more southerly waters near the mainland of Chukota.

In the summer, the dense fields of drifting ice near Wrangel form an optimum environment for mother walruses and their calves. Not only does the ice protect them from hunting ships—those super-predators against which walruses have only one defense, to escape behind pack ice—but it also provides them with the opportunity to form small resting groups on different pieces of ice. By distributing themselves over a large area, the animals reduce both their impact on food resources and social stress. A few remain in polynyas around

Above: Arctic fox, Wrangel Island
A young female Arctic fox (*Alopex lagopus*) rests on a small island of gravel amid the snow-covered landscape. Even on a calm, sunny autumn day, the fox wraps its tail around itself for warmth.

Left: Black-legged kittiwakes, Wrangel Island
In early spring, the coastal cliffs of Wrangel are silent, but at the end of April, reckless flocks of birds arrive to breed, filling the crystal clear Arctic air with unceasing hubbub. This nesting kittiwake (*Rissa tridactyla*) couple is one of eight marine bird species that breed on these cliffs, drawn to the island by the rich variety of fish in the relatively shallow sea waters.

Surrounding ice floes, Wrangel Island

The seemingly lifeless floes of ice in the sea around Wrangel Island are in fact a flexible, permanently moving extension of the islands, a living "landscape" for wandering polar bears and arctic foxes. This is the southwestern coast of Wrangel Island in early autumn, the time of year when the ocean starts to freeze.

Wrangel throughout the winter months as well. When there is no ice, the walruses usually haul out on spits at the southern and southwestern coasts of the island—Doubtful Spit and Cape Blossom—forming coastal rookeries of tens of thousands of animals.

In the winter and spring, polar bears of both sexes and all ages hunt seals on the ice in the vicinity of the islands. Every summer, the pack ice surrounding the islands begins to break into ice floes. By July, Wrangel is usually surrounded by individual ice floes or compressed fields of ice floes. Depending on the year, by late summer and through the autumn, the ice cover around the island may be sparse, and every three to four years it may be almost non-existent.

As long as there is some solid "ground" in the sea, the polar bears remain out on the ice, coming back to shore only occasionally to scout along the coastline for food or to cross the interior to get from one side of the island to the other. The bears stay on land in large numbers and for longer periods of time only when the ice melts or breaks off and drifts away to leave open sea for tens of miles around the island. When this happens, the polar bears come to shore and wait on the beach for the ice to return.

Wrangel and Herald Islands are key breeding habitats for the polar bears that roam the Chukchi and Bering Seas. About 350 to 500 pregnant bears, or 80 percent of all breeding females of the Chukchi Sea population, den on the islands. In certain areas, there are as many as

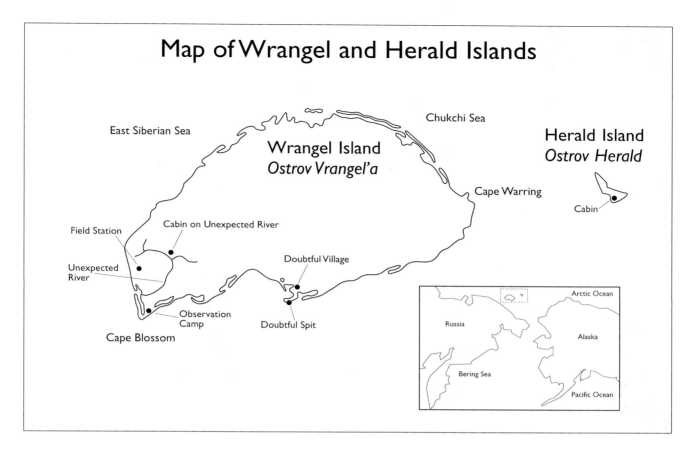

Map of Wrangel and Herald Islands

Chukchi Sea

East Siberian Sea

Wrangel Island
Ostrov Vrangel'a

Herald Island
Ostrov Herald

Cape Warring

Cabin

Field Station

Cabin on Unexpected River

Doubtful Village

Unexpected River

Observation Camp

Doubtful Spit

Cape Blossom

Arctic Ocean

Russia

Alaska

Bering Sea

Pacific Ocean

nine to nineteen dens per square mile (six to twelve dens per km²), with the highest density recorded on Herald Island. The end of October and the beginning of November are a time of high denning activity in the mountainous areas close to the shore on both islands. Only pregnant bears come to shore to hibernate. All the others—mature males, females accompanied by older cubs, and subadults—continue to hunt out on the ice during the winter. They hibernate only for short periods to survive particularly severe conditions.

Pregnant bears give birth to their cubs in the darkest months of the year, December and January. The females and their cubs remain in their snow dens until March or April, although a few may emerge as early as the end of February. All winter long the females remain under the snow, living off their fat deposits laid down during the previous summer hunting season. As soon as their cubs are strong enough, the mother bears set out for the ice. By the end of April, the dens are deserted.

In spring, the coastal areas of Herald and Wrangel and the sea ice between the islands is populated by courting and breeding bears. The mature males, which have been hunting on the ice all winter long, are particularly massive at this time, and all their attentions are concentrated on finding a female in heat. They have no interest in the lactating females, who—unless they lose their cubs—come into heat only every second year, after their cubs are old enough to fend for themselves.

Overleaf: Jagged cliffs and icy coastline, Cape Warring, Wrangel Island
While the southern and northern coasts of Wrangel are flat, the eastern and western coasts are rocky. Cape Warring is the northeastern tip of Wrangel and one of the island's most important areas for polar bear denning. Every year, several dozen female bears make their snow dens in the mountains here and settle in for hibernation. Even in summer, as pictured here, deep snow fills the narrow hollows and steep slopes of Cape Warring; the first autumn blizzards provide optimal denning habitat for pregnant females.

Wrangel and Herald Islands are key breeding habitats for the polar bears with about 350 to 500 pregnant bears denning on the islands.

Wrangel Island is named after Arctic explorer Ferdinant von Vrangel'a who was the first European to learn of the island's existence. Ironically, however, he never saw the island that bears his name.

Castellea flowers, Wrangel Island
Vegetation is especially rich along river valleys in the island's interior, which are protected by high mountains from the cold Arctic winds. In summer, temperatures may reach 68–77°F (20–25°C) in these central areas, allowing flowers such as this castellea (*Castilleja elegans*) to flourish.

The Discovery of Wrangel Island

Ostrov Vrangel'a or Wrangel Island is named after Arctic explorer and Russian Navy Lieutenant Ferdinant Petrovitch von Vrangel'a who was the first European to learn of the island's existence. Ironically, however, Vrangel'a never saw the island that bears his name.

The explorer heard of the island's existence from the Chukchi Native People of Chukotka and vowed to find the land. During the three consecutive seasons of 1821–1823, Vrangel'a made journeys by sled over the sea ice from the Siberian mainland, but bad weather held him back from attaining his goal.

In April 1823, he approached within forty to fifty miles (64–80 km) of the island but still could not see land. In 1840, he published an account of his travels, *Narrative of an Expedition to the Polar Sea in the Years 1820, 1821, 1822, and 1823*, in which he told of the frustration of his ultimate attempt: "With a painful feeling of the impossibility of overcoming the obstacles which nature opposed to us, our last hope vanished of discovering the land which we yet believed to exist. . . . We had done what duty and honor demanded; further attempts would have been absolutely hopeless, and I decided to return." Baron Vrangel'a eventually became the last Russian governor of Alaska before it was sold to the United States.

It was an American who first landed on Vrangel'a's long-sought land. In 1867, several American whaling ships were cruising to the north of the Bering Straits when one skipper, Captain Thomas Long, came in sight of an uncharted island. Being familiar with Vrangel'a's expeditions, Long named the island after him, fixed the coordinates, and added Wrangel Island to our maps.

Circumpolar Polar Bear Range

Southernmost border of regular polar bear meetings

Northern and southernmost regions of high density polar bear populations

● Remote sightings of polar bears

Rocky castle in the Arctic, Herald Island
Along with Wrangel, Ostrov Herald, known in English as Herald Island, is an important breeding habitat for polar bears in Siberian Arctic. Situated almost due east from Wrangel toward the Bering Strait and Alaska, Herald is a rocky castle of an island encircled by daunting cliffs, most of which, such as these on the southern coast, are impregnable. Female bears climb up the towering rock face of the southern coast in a few select hollows when it is covered by ice in autumn. On the top terraces, they find snow conditions that are perfect for denning.

The tiny Herald Island was, in fact, discovered almost twenty years before the large Wrangel Island.

The Discovery of Herald Island

The tiny Ostrov Herald or Herald Island was, in fact, discovered almost twenty years before the larger Wrangel Island.

In 1849, during one of the expeditions in search of the lost British explorer Sir John Franklin, Captain Henry Kellet reached a small uncharted island and landed on August 6. He named the island after his ship, HMS *Herald*.

From the top of Herald Island, the *Herald*'s crew also sighted mountaintops to the west and north, which Kellet thought to be several small islands with an extensive land beyond. This larger landmass was placed on Admiralty Charts as "Kellett's Land" or "Mountains seen from Herald," but Kellet had not bothered to fix the coordinates. Unbeknownst to him, Kellet had actually sighted what would later be called Wrangel Island.

Circumpolar Polar Bear Denning Sites

Sea of Okhotsk

Bering Sea

Pacific Ocean

Gulf of Alaska

Chukchi Sea

Herald Island

Wrangle Island

East Siberian Sea

Laptev Sea

RUSSIA

Karaskoye More

Arctic Ocean

North Pole

Beaufort Sea

Barents Sea

CANADA

Baffin Bay

Greenland Sea

Norwegian Sea

Denmark Strait

North Sea

Hudson Bay

Davis Strait

Atlantic Ocean

Polar bear denning sites

Both photos: Reindeer and musk-oxen, Wrangel Island

On the coast of Wrangel, polar bears share habitat with reindeer (*Rangifer tarandus tarandus*) and musk-oxen (*Ovibos moschatus*), but only occasionally does a bear try to hunt these ungulates. Both reindeer and musk-oxen are too fast for polar bears to prey upon as the bears quickly overheat during the chase. Neither reindeer nor musk-oxen are native to Wrangel: humans introduced reindeer in the early 1950s and musk-oxen in 1975.

When I set out for Wrangel, I had no idea how many polar bears I would meet. I was completely unprepared for what I was to encounter.

Courting continues from the end of March until May. A courting couple stays together for several days, during which time they copulate a number of times. They then go their separate ways.

The embryo does not begin to grow until after the summer hunting season and the female has built her maternity den. If she fails to find enough food during the summer, the embryo will be reabsorbed. Polar bear mothers have from one to three cubs per litter, with the older and younger females having the smallest litters.

The polar bear spends most of its life out on the ice searching for food over an enormous expanse of territory. A marine mammal, it is at home in a world of sea and ice where it is difficult for the researcher to follow. Even though polar bears have been studied for extensive periods of time, our knowledge of their biology is poor, and we know even less about their social interactions and behavior in the wild. When I undertook my research, I decided to concentrate on three areas: the social life of polar bears, the way polar bears interact with their prey, and the behavior of mother bears in their secluded denning areas.

When I set out for my first autumn of observation on Wrangel, I had no idea how much bear activity I would be able to observe or how best to work with the bears. I only knew that polar bears visit the island in the autumn and that if I was in the right place at the right time, I might be able to learn something.

As it turned out, I was completely unprepared for what I was to encounter.

Chapter 1

The Adventure Begins

My first season with polar bears on Wrangel Island was in 1990. The climatic conditions that autumn were unusual for the Arctic, and especially for the Wrangel Island region. Only rarely in the recorded history of the island have there been years when the drifting pack ice has melted so much that the island is almost completely surrounded by open water. In normal years, there is ice all around the island. Even in warm years, you can expect solid ice at least along the north coast, but in late August 1990, the southern edge of the drifting pack ice was 120 miles (200 km) north of the northern coast, and the last small field of broken ice near the southern coast disappeared on August 27.

By the first week of September, the pack ice had moved even farther to the north—some 300 miles (500 km) in all—and it was not until the middle of October that it started to move back. Right up to the end of that month, there was no ice to be found throughout the vast marine area from Wrangel east to Alaska and west to the Taimyr Peninsula, 1,200 miles (2,000 km) away. As a result, hundreds of polar bears lost their drifting hunting grounds and got stuck on Wrangel Island. Some wandered along the coast and inland searching for something to eat, but most congregated at the only practical food source, the walrus rookeries.

Parade of polar bears, Cape Blossom
Walking in a neat and orderly single-file line, this parade of polar bears makes its way along the beach to Cape Blossom directly in front of our cabin on Wrangel. Cape Blossom has long been a walrus breeding rookery and also attracts hungry polar bears—sometimes by the dozens. This is a polar bear family group: a mother with her two two-year-old cubs. Only mature, experienced females can successfully raise a litter of three, although a three-cub litter is not unusual in the Wrangel region. I called the mom, right, Marfa. Her two female cubs bring up the rear.

Hundreds of polar bears wandered along the coast, searching for food at the walrus rookeries.

When the walrus arrive at Wrangel, if there is no ice to rest on, the animals collect into large herds and start to haul out on the beach. In 1990, a total of 130,000 walruses were summering within the Wrangel and Herald Island area, and at least seven different locations on the beaches of both islands were temporarily occupied by their rookeries. By autumn, several more rookeries had formed along the coast of Wrangel, even in places where walruses had not hauled out since the 1950s and 1960s. Both polar bears and walruses found themselves in a difficult situation that year, and if there was any good luck at all, it was mine: I was exceptionally fortunate to witness this rare event.

My destination that autumn was Cape Blossom, an outstanding place even in this unique area of the Arctic. On the map, Wrangel Island looks like a polar bear skull. Cape Blossom is a "fang" aimed toward the mainland where a gravel spit surrounded by water on three sides penetrates deep into the sea. Here polar bears can rest on solid ground while comfortably close to their native environment. The cape has long been host to walrus rookeries, and their remains attract polar bears even when there are no live walruses on the beach.

My journey to Cape Blossom was long and hard. The purpose of my trip was not only to watch polar bears but also to film them for the BBC nature series *Realms of the Russian Bear.* My companion on this expedition was Hugh Maynard, a cameraman from the BBC Natural History Unit. Personally, filming was secondary to the observations I

Spring on Wrangel Island

Top: Fed by the Unknown River, this is the heart of Wrangel in advanced spring. The central regions of the island are warmer than the coast, providing a longer growing season for Arctic flowers.

Above: Dryad (*Dryas punctata*)

Left: One of the seventeen species of Arctic poppies (*Papaver*) on Wrangel, of which there are five endemic species.

I hoped to observe polar bears and walruses, as little is known about the interactions between these two giants of the Arctic.

Observation camp, Cape Blossom
The log cabins on Cape Blossom that I used as a polar bear observation camp were originally built in the sixties to serve as a seasonal weather station.

hoped to make of polar bears and walruses in the area. Little is known about the interactions between these two giants of the Arctic, and I hoped to find out more about their relationship. With ice conditions the way they were, my hopes were high.

On September 9, 1990, we started out early from Doubtful Village, a settlement on the south coast of Wrangel. Our all-terrain vehicle was overloaded with camera equipment and food, and we made slow progress over the harsh, stony terrain. By the end of the first day, we had covered about forty-eight miles (80 km) and were still some twenty-four miles (40 km) from our destination, a log cabin on Cape Blossom that had been built in the sixties as a seasonal polar weather station. The cabin was now a field camp for the Wrangel Island nature reserve, but it was rarely used.

We spent the first night at a cabin on the upper reaches of Unexpected River which in former times had been used by reindeer herders. The next morning we made another early start. The cold wind that had been blowing snowy clouds over the mountain ridge to the north all night long continued on into the morning. The first touch of winter had already whitened the high ground. As we descended the river valley, we found the foliage still yellowish-brown and the air warm. The wind weakened and then died. The heady smell of withered Arctic flowers and willow leaves surrounded us, and the air grew hazy from the heat of the sun. We basked in the brief moment of Indian summer for we knew that Arctic winter was on its way and that cold winds and snow might strike at any time. The days were getting significantly shorter, and we knew we would have short days at the end of the trip to work with the bears.

Along the river bank we filmed a pregnant polar bear relaxing in the grass at the foot of hill as she waited for snow so she could build her den. By the time we reached the coast it was late, and the sun was already low in the sky. The sea was open with not a single ice floe in sight. We still had to drive along the shore of the lagoon for five miles (8 km) to get to the cabin. The gentle southern breeze carried the barking of thousands of walruses. Cape Blossom sounded promising, and we were getting excited.

~

The first polar bear we came across after we left the river valley was on the beach five miles (4 km) from the cabin. It was a female with one cub-of-the-year (a cub born within the last twelve months). The pair was ambling toward the cape when we rounded a hillock to find them only 100 feet (30 m) away from us. They were even more surprised than we were. The mother rushed her cub into the water and escaped to the long gravel spit on the other side of the shallow lagoon.

After that encounter, bears crossed our path with increasing frequency. Next, we encountered a mature male who followed the

On the road to Cape Blossom
I pilot an ATV loaded down with supplies along the main "road" to the observation cabin. Our trip to Cape Blossom was a two-day ride, and we spent the night in an old reindeer herders' cabin on the Unexpected River.

example of the first family; then came a mother with two cubs, followed in rapid succession by a single bear. We had had the cabin in our sights for the past half an hour, but I was reluctant to approach it over open ground. Finally, we came to a spot where we could drive up to the cabin under the shelter of higher ground to make our approach as unobtrusively as possible.

I turned the ATV around the slope, drove up the coastal hillock toward the cabin, and stopped in surprise—our way was blocked by at least six mature polar bears. They seemed agitated and scarcely acknowledged our presence. On the beach behind the cabin, walruses were barking. I edged the ATV forward and stopped, keeping the engine running. A huge male bear approached us, sniffing the air.

I hesitated. The cabin was only eighty feet (25 m) from the beach, and I did not know whether the walruses were basking on the shore or swimming in the sea. I did not want to drive up to the cabin door for fear I might disturb the walruses if they were on the beach, but there was no way to reach the cabin on foot without getting mixed up with the polar bears. I was still hesitating when the bear took the initiative and walked toward us. His approach forced me to react, and I circled in front of him with the ATV. He stopped and watched us for some time before getting worried and leaving the scene. The other bears scattered. The way to the cabin was now clear, but I suspected it would not be long before the bears returned.

Darkness was falling fast, and we had no time to investigate what

Snowy owls, Wrangel Island
A female snowy owl (*Nyctea scandiaca*) carries a lemming clutched in her claws to her ground nest as dinner for her recently hatched chicks.

the bears who had greeted us were doing now that they had abandoned the cabin. Leaving the ATV, we walked to the cabin and looked out to the beach beyond. An amazing sight met our eyes: tens of thousands of walruses were churning up the sea. They were all in the water, which meant we could drive the ATV right up to the cabin without fear of disturbing them. Eager to unload before the bears drifted back, we rushed to the ATV, and I drove it up to the door. We hurried to get our food and equipment inside, and I parked the ATV in a shed near the cabin, hidden away from prying polar bear eyes.

When the cabin at Cape Blossom is not in use, wooden shutters cover the windows to prevent the bears from breaking the glass and adopting the dwelling for themselves. The first thing Hugh and I did to make the place habitable was to open the shutters to let in the dying light of day. It did not take long for the bears to decide to drop by to see what was happening. As long as we were on the ATV with the engine running, the bears were cautious and kept their distance. Now that we were safely inside the cabin, they became more assertive.

Hugh was busy with his cameras, and I was attaching our field radio to the wall when I heard a knocking on the window six feet (2 m) to my right. I glanced across to see the large head of a mature female polar bear. She was smelling the glass and trying to get a look at what was going on inside. Two curious cubs-of-the-year were stamping their feet anxiously behind her. I jumped to the window and, without

thinking, tapped on the glass right in front of her wet nose. The results exceeded my expectations. The bear recoiled and disappeared around the corner of the cabin followed by her two obedient cubs.

I returned to my exercise with the radio, but in less than two minutes I was interrupted again. This time it was a single bear knocking on the kitchen window. I jumped up and got rid of him using the same tactic I had used with the mother bear. After that I could not stick with the radio for more than a minute. There were bears swarming all around the cabin wanting to find out what had happened when they had been forced—temporarily—to abandon camp.

One by one the bears approached the cabin investigating one window after another. Sometimes there was knocking on two windows simultaneously. We had no choice but to jump from window to window to scare the bears away. Neither of us relished the thought of having to sleep in a cabin open to the chill winds of the Arctic autumn. "This is no good," I said to Hugh after a while. "We have to close the shutters." Hugh, to his credit and my relief, agreed to accompany me outside.

~

We came out of the cabin together. There were two bears in front of the door and more were hanging around. We could not see much in the twilight, but we could see that the bears were excited. When the bears closest to the doorway saw us, they took fright, and we had no

Polar bear "herd," Cape Blossom
Making my way to Cape Blossom in autumn for the first time, I knew that polar bears liked the spot, and I might have a good chance to find at least a few animals there. I could not believe my eyes when to my surprise, I found what can only be called a "herd" of these "solitary" white bears on the shore. Now I had to decide how to deal with this crowd.

I heard a knocking on the cabin window and glanced across to see the large head of a female polar bear looking inside.

problem closing the shutters. We were confused for a moment when a mature female and her two cubs suddenly jumped up the small ridge above the beach only sixty feet (20 m) in front of us; however, the next moment it became clear that she was confused, too, and she simply led her cubs away.

With the shutters closed and the oil lamps on, the cabin became our castle. We were now more comfortable, but the drawback was that we could not see what was going on outside. Shut off from the bears, neither of us could relax as we drank our evening tea. Apart from the fact that our curiosity was killing us, we could not enjoy our safe haven because two essential resources were outside—our source of fresh water and the toilet—and we needed more wood for the stove. So, after finishing our tea, we decided to venture out again.

"Look at that," said Hugh sharply, aiming his flashlight to the left of the cabin. The face of the big polar bear appeared from around the corner only ten feet (3 m) away as we collected driftwood in front of the cabin door. The bear stared at the light, noisily smelling the air. It was a female, a mature and massive animal, and her face was covered in blood from her ears to her neck. The long sunset of Arctic autumn was over, and Cape Blossom was wrapped in darkness. The bear was not alone. Two cubs clung to her, one on either side, seeming to find courage by flattening themselves against her. Their faces, too, were bloodstained. The picture was impressive: three bloody polar bear heads in a row within the circle of light, just a few yards away from us.

The female, breathing nervously, moved forward two steps, and the cubs followed as though glued to her. The bear hissed at us and then made a snorting sound. She obviously could not see well in the darkness but felt compelled to investigate. Here were two strangers in her usual range, and she was curious and anxious. As she narrowed the distance between us, I thought the situation was getting too risky—for both sides. I stepped toward her making a threat display—a sharp feint as though I intended to hit or bite her—and then I struck the ground just in front of her with the shovel I was carrying for protection. We had no weapons with us, and I had intuitively grabbed the shovel, feeling that I needed to have something in my hands to create an imaginary barrier between me and the bear.

The female hesitated for a second, hissed at me, and then turned back. Nudging her cubs and calling them to follow, she ran away. Hugh, who had been standing beside me the whole time holding the flashlight, flicked the beam to the other side of the cabin where yet another bear was peering at us from around the corner. This bear was not big and it was alone. Like the female we had just chased away, it, too, had a bloodstained face. Again we went through the motions of curiosity, confrontation, and withdrawal. That was as much as we could take for now. We grabbed a supply of wood and water, and went inside and bolted the door.

Visitor at the window, Cape Blossom
Wooden shutters protected the windows of the cabin when not in use, but as soon as we removed them and settled in, we had curious polar bears knocking at the window, wondering about their new neighbors. Curiosity is a natural instinct of the white bears and should not be mistaken for a predatory, mankiller instinct.

The face of a big polar bear appeared around the corner, her face covered in blood from her ears to her neck. And the bear was not alone.

Despite that somewhat unnerving experience, once back inside the cabin we could not sit behind four walls separated from the life outside for long. Throughout that evening, whenever either of us looked outside, we saw at least one polar bear and often several. They were around the cabin all the time, passing by or jumping down the little cliff to the beach. They sometimes hissed at us or ran away, but they never tried to attack us, even when we left the safety of the cabin. As we prepared our evening meal, we could hear them rubbing their noses against the wooden shutters and sniffing loudly, presumably trying to make sense of the smell of these two strangers and the food they were cooking. By now we had acclimatized somewhat. Although the bears surrounded the cabin, they did not seem to be trying to break in. We had no guns or rifles, but we retired to bed that night confident that the bears would not give us cause to use them anyway.

Falling asleep, I thought of the polar bears continuing their night life on the other side of the cabin walls. I also reflected how lucky I was to have Hugh as my companion. At no time was he to disappoint me or to give me cause to doubt his confidence in my ability to manage the bears. In all our time together, there was to be just one point on which we did not see eye to eye. Every morning, Hugh would be up before me impeccably dressed, clean shaven, and drinking his morning cup of tea in preparation for following me wherever I would lead him among the bears. Every morning, he boiled up just enough water for his cup of tea, and every morning, I had to struggle with the old gas heater to prepare mine. No matter what tactic I tried, I just could not get him to break with his established habit of preparing a cup of tea for one. I found solace in the thought that Hugh conformed to my impression of what an English gentleman should be—brave, precise, and conservative.

~

The next morning, Hugh and I inspected the area for the first time in daylight. Now it became clear why the polar bears had been so excited during the night. The fresh remains of a walrus calf lay on the ground not more than fifty feet (15 m) from our door. The bears had had a successful hunt, and we had gotten a piece of the action. The beach was empty now, but tracks on the gravel indicated intense activity by both polar bears and walruses. Strung out along the coast, thousands of walruses were in the water as far as the eye could see. Polar bears were everywhere. I counted 87 adults within just over one mile (2 km) of the cabin. A week later, from the height of the Cape Blossom reflector tower—a log tower with a sheet of metal at the top to reflect locator signals sent out from passing ships—I counted 122 adults and 18 cubs.

I had known that Cape Blossom was one of the best places in the world to observe polar bears, but I had never expected to find such a huge number of them in such a small area. I was not ready for this, but now that we were here, I had to find a way to work with this mass of bears.

Uninvited—but expected—guests, Cape Blossom

Our cabin was right along the route the polar bears walked to Cape Blossom for walrus hunting, so the white bears naturally stopped in to check us out once they sensed the presence of man in their domain. The doorway to our cold-room always attracted the attention of these visitors who were prone to investigate any and all buildings. The novel scent of human beings seemed to be a warning signal, but also an open invitation to the bears to come visit. Some of our curious guests could not resist the attractive smell and just had to take a souvenir with them from our cold room.

Chapter 2

A Spit Full of Bears

At Cape Blossom I was privileged to live and work in an area where, in certain months, polar bears are the most numerous animals around. I also had the good fortune to undertake my observations during four years when ice was largely absent from the surrounding sea, forcing the bears onto Wrangel Island. The length of the ice-free periods varied from year to year. In 1990, it was eight weeks; it was four weeks in 1991; about two weeks in 1992; and six and a half weeks in 1993. The number of bears and walruses and their interactions were different every year. What did not change was my luck. Every year I witnessed high concentrations of polar bears on the shore. In 1990, 140 animals were gathered in the observation area at one time. In 1991, there were 37. There were 12 in 1992 and 39 in 1993.

When I was first greeted at Cape Blossom by a mass of hungry polar bears around the cabin, it took me just one evening to recognize that I had two alternatives: I could sit in the cabin and separate myself completely from the bears or I could find a way to live among them. I chose the latter approach and set to work to develop a method of interacting with them.

Polar bears and walruses on the spit, Cape Blossom
Hungry polar bears bask in the autumn sunshine on the gravel beach of Cape Blossom. Offshore, a multitude of walruses float in the surf, wary of hauling out on the spit while their chief predator is at hand.

Inquisitve female, Cape Blossom

Living in the cabin surrounded by dozens of polar bears, I simply could not avoid their attention. Walking among them on the cape, I frequently met the white bears. The summer hunting season had been good for this well-fed female surveying the spit filled with walruses. Polar bears are so well insulated by their thick fur and a layer of blubber that can measure 1½ inches (4 cm) thick over their muscles and up to 4¾ inches (12 cm) thick on their rump that they experience little heat loss even in the dead of an Arctic winter.

I did not intend to carry a weapon when I was among the polar bears. I wanted to be able to interact with them as one animal to another.

Humans may be superpredators when they are armed, but polar bears are the largest non-aquatic carnivores in the world. A well-fed, healthy, mature adult male in the Bering Sea can weigh on average from 880 to 1,540 pounds (400–700 kg) and can kill a full-grown seal with one swipe of his mighty paw. These were the animals I wanted to get to know, and I did not intend to carry a weapon when I was among them. I wanted to be able to interact with the bears as one animal to another.

My initial theory was simple: When with polar bears, do as polar bears do. They are wild animals living close to nature, I reasoned, not human beings operating in an artificial urban environment. Although human beings can lose touch with the world around them and act in an unpredictable fashion, wild animals cannot be crazy if they are to survive. They simply have to have a normal instinct for self-preservation. This means they have to be always on their guard, avoiding objects and situations that could be dangerous.

To minimize the risk of being attacked by the bears, I decided that I should show them that I, too, am an animal to be feared and respected. I felt the bears would keep their distance if I walked among them in a confident, aggressive manner, feeling psychologically ready to attack any bear at any time. Even though I had no previous experience with polar bears in the wild, I believed that the bears would feel the same way I would—uneasy, cautious, and perhaps even frightened—if I

were approached by a large, dark stranger. As long as I can move confidently among them, I thought, and as long as I do not turn my back on them, they will be suspicious and fearful and will not risk attacking me. Based on what I knew about animal behavior, I decided to act as though I were a bear of the highest social rank, untouchable within polar bear society. To execute this plan, I had to watch the bears closely to learn more about their social interactions and to learn to interpret their moods.

For my method to succeed, the bears must always believe that I am dominant and could be a threat to them at any time. This was important for my own safety, but it was in the bears' interests, too. Bears are intelligent animals with good memories. Once one is trained to be careful with humans, to keep its distance and not to get too familiar, it is more likely to survive future encounters with hunters or with anyone else who might kill a bear.

Well, I thought, the theory sounds persuasive enough—but how will it work in practice?

~

The morning after our arrival at Cape Blossom, life was going on, and polar bears were milling around the cabin. I decided it was time to test the theory. I thought it would take too long and be too difficult to explain all my theoretical points to Hugh, so I simply recommended that he follow my instructions precisely. Fully recov-

Walrus rookery, Wrangel Island
An adult female walrus wades in to shore, ready to haul out as a massive rookery forms on the spit. Every year about mid-July, walruses arrive on the coast of Wrangel to spend the summer in the shallow waters surrounding the island. Coastal rookeries with tens of thousands of walruses on the beach send a strong signal seaward with loud barking and a strong scent beckoning other walruses. The rookery continues to grow at both sides while in the middle, the mass of walruses is mostly relaxed. To make room for themselves on the beach, walruses often use their tusks to force neighbors aside.

My initial theory was simple: When with polar bears, do as polar bears do.

ered by now from his encounters with bears the night before, the ever-amicable Hugh agreed to accompany me outside.

I first tested my theory on five bears who were feeding on the remains of a walrus calf that had been left in the tundra 650 feet (200 m) to the east of the cabin the night before. When we approached them with our cameras, there were two mothers with cubs and a subadult around the carcass. As I expected, they all ran away as soon as they could make out that two strangers in dark clothing were approaching them. Turning back toward the cabin, we met a lone bear with bloodstained fur who seemed satisfied and happy after his morning meal. He looked at us with lazy curiosity as we approached to within forty feet (12 m). Only then did he get a little frightened and run away. The initial results were promising and my confidence was building; however, the major test was yet to come.

There were still polar bears all around the cabin, but the greatest concentration of animals was on the gravel spit on the western side of the peninsula. Every day we could see dozens of bears lying on the beach or scavenging for something edible among the old bones and walrus skins that had piled up over the years at the traditional rookery sites. The average daily density of bears at Cape Blossom ranged from seven to thirty-seven animals per acre (3 to 15 animals per ha). One memorable day, I recorded thirty-eight polar bears, including young, within two and a half acres (1 ha). They were lying on their day beds, patrolling the area, and interacting with one another—and they were trying to hunt walruses, the only live prey available on land.

When I agreed to act as the scientific consultant for the Wrangel Island filming with the BBC Natural History Unit, I promised John Sparks, the series' executive producer, to do what I could to ensure that Hugh got the best possible polar bear shots. There could be no better opportunity to realize this promise than to take full advantage of the unusual density of bears and to lead Hugh right into the thick of things, to say nothing of it being another opportunity to test my theory. The conditions were good for me—as two dark figures on the gravel spit we would have plenty of room to take command of the situation—but they were also good for Hugh for he might shoot some good footage. At least that was how I justified exposing Hugh to the bears on the spit.

On the second day of our stay at Cape Blossom, after I had made an initial assessment of the situation and had tested my theory on a few more bears, I told Hugh that now was the time to approach the main concentration of bears. The wind, which had been blowing all night, dropped at about noon, and the gray sky started to clear. I explained that we would have the best chance of observing the bears if we went "straight to the top and became dominant members of the herd." Hugh accepted this without hesitation, as though I had asked him to go for a drink. He looked at the sky and commented thoughtfully that the light

Welcome to Wrangel Island
This was the first bear I met when ready to test my theory of interacting with polar bears. He was was stained in blood from head to foot after happily devouring a freshly killed walrus.

Every day we could see dozens of bears lying on the beach or scavenging for something edible among the old bones and walrus skins.

was not perfect for filming. Then, perhaps seeing my investigative fervor, he added that under such circumstances he always persuades himself that the light is "dramatic."

And so we set off, armed, as on our first evening, with just a shovel. The real test had begun. (I would never recommend that anyone repeat this test, not because I doubt the method or the temper of polar bears, but because I doubt the ability of most people to interpret bear behavior correctly. Any large predator can be dangerous in certain conditions, and it is important to be able to recognize these potentially risky situations in order to avoid them. Almost invariably when a human is injured or killed by a large predator, it is because of provocation by the human—and the result is usually a new campaign against the predator.)

While approaching the bears, I watched them carefully to keep track of their current mood, adjusting my behavior as required. Hugh was doing well following my instructions. We had no rifle because I believe that people with rifles in their hands tend to rely on the rifles rather than on themselves, and that is when mistakes happen. Do not ever consider approaching a large predator if you feel uneasy managing a close interaction on the strength of psychological superiority alone. If you do, you risk both your life and the life of the animal.

Swimming to Wrangel Island

In 1990, environmental conditions were unusual even for a season with open seas. By the beginning of September, not a single ice floe could be found within hundreds of miles of Wrangel's coast. All of the polar bears in the surrounding sea were forced to search for solid ground; this mature male bear swam many miles to reach the coast—a long, exhausting distance even for a swimmer as good as a polar bear.

We had no rifle because I believe that people with rifles in their hands tend to rely on the rifles rather than on themselves, and that is when mistakes happen.

As we walked along the peninsula on day one of our polar bear adventure, the first bears we saw were lying on their day beds looking relaxed. They noticed us at a distance of about 650 feet (200 m) and became alert. Some of them sat up and started to watch us, but we did not change course. The bears' reaction supported my theory. Before long, more than twenty of them were walking or slowly running in front of us to the top of the spit. Some escaped to either side and a few stayed put some 150 feet (50 m) away, but it seemed that all of them had conceded our dominance.

We met only one bear that day that did not back down. It was a big old male who let us pass within 130 feet (40 m) without any sign of wariness on his part. He was relaxing in a small pool of water with his muzzle beneath the surface, releasing air bubbles from his nostrils and watching the result of this exercise with rapt attention.

Our destination that day was the base of the Cape Blossom reflector tower, about one and a quarter miles (2 km) from the cabin, where we could stay among bears without being completely exposed on all sides. More than fifty male and female bears of all ages were concentrated at the end of the beach near the tower, and to reach its base, we had to open a corridor through this mass of bears. We reached our goal successfully and then tried to hide behind the base of the tower and a couple of empty fuel drums left over from some earlier expedition. We

unpacked our equipment and got to work. Some bears continued to watch us; others returned to their usual activities. We had established ourselves on bear territory and could breathe more easily—but not for long.

Once we stopped moving and were no longer troubling the bears, their natural curiosity started to overcome their fear. One by one, they approached these new creatures that had appeared under the tower. I kept having to interrupt Hugh while he was filming and simulate attacks on the bears to get them to back away. In most cases they ran as soon as they caught my scent. But a few were more highly motivated, and I had to simulate more intensive attacks to get them to run. Some were easy to drive off, even when they got within twelve to fifteen feet (4–5 m) of us, but a few were getting even closer before retreating. One mature female with a fat yearling was so eager to investigate me that I had to pretend to attack her twice before she turned and ran away.

For the next two hours, Hugh filmed bears and I pushed them away with the shovel. I barely had a chance to exchange the shovel for my camera. We would have liked to stay longer, but we headed back to the cabin when it started to get dark. We did not want to risk a close encounter with a polar bear who could not make out what we were in the darkness.

Curious bears, Cape Blossom
On their way to the spit to hunt for walrus, the mature female that I called Marfa and her three two-year-old cubs pass our camp along the beach. Recognizing the human scent, Marfa rears up on her back legs, a typical polar bear stance when it is curious and wants to see something better.

During the course of my eight seasons observing polar bears on Wrangel and Herald Islands, I had over five hundred direct exchanges with bears.

I believe if we treat polar bears with care and respect, they are far less likely to hurt us than we are to hurt them with our thoughtless and careless ways.

Above: Polar bear day beds, Cape Blossom
The white bears often make temporary day beds to rest in during the daytime, such as this one dug into the snow at the end of Cape Blossom. Male bears in particular like to make their day beds close to the water.

Opposite: White bear, Cape Blossom
The fur of the white bear is not actually white. Rather, the hairs are free of pigment and are transparent. The hairs are also hollow, which allows them to work as efficient solar collectors. The hollow hairs conduct the heat of ultraviolet light, carrying it to the bear's skin, which is black, a color ideal for absorbing radiant heat. Polar bears look white because the pigment-free fur reflects light, just as snow and ice does. A bear's winter coat can be two and a half inches (6 cm) long on its back and up to six inches (15 cm) long on its belly.

After a day spent among the bears, we felt elated. Crystal clear Arctic air, the smell of the ocean, the barks of thousands of walruses, and the press of polar bears literally breathing in our faces had gone to our heads like champagne. Now I felt sure I would be able to work with the bears even though their numbers had taken me by surprise.

Our cabin was right in the middle of the polar bears' regular trails to the beach, and many times a day bears would come up and look in through the windows or the open door. Sometimes they slept within a few dozen yards of the cabin. They never deliberately tried to damage our household or to hurt us. They seemed to accept our presence and our right to share their territory. We, in turn, respected them and made sure we did our best to minimize our impact on their activities.

The price we paid was to have walruses hauling out near, or even just in front of, our door and to have polar bears jumping on them and eating walrus kills around the outside of our home. For me, to live with the animal you are studying is the only way to learn about its life in the wild. All the hardships of spending long seasons among polar bears in the High Arctic were well worth the privilege of witnessing firsthand the private life of the mysterious ice bear.

After that year, I spent three more years living with polar bears on Wrangel and Herald Islands, sometimes with a companion but more often alone. As most of my observations were based on face-to-face encounters with bears, I started to focus on practical ways to manage interactions between human beings and polar bears. The system I developed is based on my observation of polar bears interacting with one another and of the defensive methods used by walruses against attacking bears; however, I have always clearly understood that the apparent ease of my dealings with polar bears should not be taken for granted. Each bear has its own personality and, as with any highly developed species, each individual animal may behave differently under different circumstances. Every meeting I had with bears was handled with the utmost concern both for my safety and for the safety of the animal.

During the course of my eight seasons observing polar bears on Wrangel and Herald Islands, I had over five hundred direct exchanges with bears, and each exchange was unique. Taken together, the exchanges proved to my satisfaction that the principles I developed during my first season with polar bears were sound. Of course, I refined my techniques as I learned more about bears—there is always room for improvement—but I never learned anything that caused me to doubt that it is possible to live peacefully in a cabin surrounded by tens of bears, or that it is possible to walk among them if you have to. You just need to have steady nerves and an intimate knowledge of the rules that govern their social behavior. I believe if we treat polar bears with care and respect, they are far less likely to hurt us than we are to hurt them with our thoughtless and careless ways.

Chapter 3

A Singular Bear

There is one special pleasure for me in the behavioral study of animals in the wild—getting to know animal personalities. It did not take me long to realize that the bigger the wild animal, the more exciting it is for me to get to know it up close and personal.

Before I turned to polar bears, I had spent twelve years studying Arctic foxes. They are intelligent and resourceful little creatures, and I never tired of watching them. I followed their daily lives with empathy, but as an observer and not as a participant. Because of our size difference, interactions with foxes did not involve me as a partner.

With polar bears it was different. We were about the same size—although the bears are heavier and more powerful—and each interaction forced me to play a kind of game in which I had to adjust myself to the bears' social etiquette. In other words, I had to play at being a polar bear. Never before had I had such pleasure interacting with animals.

Female and cub come to visit, Cape Blossom
Female polar bears are good mothers. They take care to avoid risky situations and would bravely protect their cubs if necessary. This mother bear came to visit our camp but hesitated in getting too close to our cabin. When she recognized the presence of nearby humans, she stopped for a moment in confusion before choosing to retreat from our foreign scent in order to protect her cub. In dangerous situations, cubs hide behind their mothers; however, being curious about unknown things, they often peek around their mothers for a better look.

To really get familiar with a polar bear, you need to meet it up close.

Snowy owls and camp, Cape Blossom
Every autumn, a mass of migrating snowy owls arrives at Cape Blossom from inner parts of the island. Usually the birds spend a few days flying over the coast and hunting for food before they take wing to continue their migration south. Seasons with long open-sea periods and severe storms are extremely hard on the snowy owls; during these times, they concentrate at Cape Blossom in great numbers and wait as long as needed for optimal conditions before crossing the strait to the Siberian mainland.

At Cape Blossom in 1990, polar bears came up to the cabin many times a day. Even staying close to home I could meet many different bears face to face. For the first three days, Hugh and I were alone, then we were joined by Igor Oleinikov and Anatoli (Tolya) Kochnev. Igor had come to observe seabirds and Tolya was there to study the structure of the walrus rookery. The polar bears soon learned that more strangers had arrived whose rights they had to take into account; the new arrivals, for their part, treated the bears as we did, and the bears continued their frequent visits to the cabin.

It is not difficult to identify individual bears by their appearance and patterns of behavior. I was soon able to distinguish many individuals. I learned to read their moods and intentions, and I could nearly always adjust my behavior accordingly. There was one bear, however, that I never could understand. Perhaps he was the bear who was lying in the pool of water blowing air bubbles with his nose when Hugh and I first walked out among the bears. Perhaps he was the one who let us pass close by him while the others were running away. I do not know because I did not get a good look at him at the time. To get really familiar with a polar bear, you need to meet it up close. The first time I got close to my mysterious bear was September 16, 1990.

The previous day a severe snowstorm had pushed a great number of snowy owls from the foothills to the coast. By afternoon a wave of migrating owls had rolled down the valley, and by dusk, hundreds of owls were sitting like small columns on the tundra, on the spit, and on the beach. The wind died out in the night, and the next day dawned bright, frosty, and calm. Winter had finally wrapped the island in its icy embrace. Walruses, which had taken refuge in the open ocean during the storm's fury, were returning to shore. We watched thousands of them swimming along the beach in front of our cabin. A hundred yards to the east they were already hauling out, and the rookery was rapidly spreading westward.

We were just finishing our breakfast as the walruses formed a new "wedge" of the rookery in front of the cabin. The animals were anxious to rest after several exhausting days at sea. The air was full of walrus barks, and the water was seething with walrus bodies. Soon the wedge nearest to us spilled over into neighboring wedges, and they all joined up with the main rookery, which now stretched some one and a quarter miles (2 km) along the beach. From the cabin we could see tens of thousands walruses on land and in the water. Walruses are especially nervous when they haul out. They are prone to panic and often rush back into the sea for no apparent reason. As small a disturbance as a low-flying seagull can turn a forming rookery back into the water. Once the rookery has formed and the walruses have settled, however, they are not so easily dislodged. Even a polar bear would be

hard pressed to rout a stable rookery.

That morning, I was sitting eighty feet (25 m) from the cabin door behind a couple of empty fuel drums that served as a simple blind. I was watching the rookery form, when suddenly walruses at the far end of the beach started to panic. The panic spread rapidly. It took me a moment to realize what was happening. And then I understood. A huge bear, a mature male, appeared from behind the ridge at the opposite end of the beach from my blind. He was walking slowly toward my end of the rookery, ignoring the barking walruses around him.

The bear did not look hungry and perhaps it was too warm for him to hurry. He looked fat and healthy. His face was stained with a mixture of fresh blood and sand, a sign that he had eaten just a short while ago. He was not the tallest male I have ever seen, but he was massive. He was full of power, confidence, and dignity. As he walked, he pushed his forelegs out to the side as all bears do. For him, however, this regal gait just strengthened the image of superiority. As he came nearer, I saw he had a large scar on the right side of his upper lip that made him look as though he was grinning disdainfully. The massive bear hardly noticed the walruses, who were now leaving the beach in droves, clearing a path before him. He simply walked along, sniffing the gravel and looking at the beach. He came up to the ridge, ate some snow, and continued his walk. A smaller male followed him on a path above the beach. Both bears were approaching my observation point.

When he was 130 feet (40 m) from my rudimentary blind, the

Inquisitive bear, Cape Blossom
Curiosity overcomes fear, and this white bear cautiously sniffs an outside wall of one of our cabins. Garbage left in the camp from former expeditions attracted the bears in droves, so when I first occupied the cabins in 1990, one of the first things to do was to clean the territory around the camp.

Grandfather was a huge bear, a mature male, full of power, confidence, and dignity. He had a large scar on his upper lip that made him look as though he was grinning disdainfully.

Grandfather continued to advance, ignoring me. By now I was getting used to commanding more respect from the bears. My uneasiness grew, and it became clear this was no time to be taking pictures.

Grandfather, Cape Blossom

Getting to know the personality of individual polar bears is a special pleasure for me in the behavioral study of animals in the wild. This bear I called Grandfather, and he stood out from all the other white bears I have seen. When I first saw him, his face was stained with fresh blood. He was massive, full of power, confidence, and dignity—and he did not hesitate in walking straight toward me.

massive male climbed the ridge and headed toward me. He seemed to have chosen the upper trail to get a better view of our camp. I decided to take a picture of this impressive specimen. To get a better view, I got out of the blind (if a couple of fuel drums may be considered a blind) and lay down on the ground. When the bear was within sixty feet or so (20 m), I took the picture.

The bear continued to advance, ignoring me completely. I found that strange. By now I was getting used to commanding more respect from the bears. My uneasiness grew as he continued his relentless advance. It was becoming clear that this was no time to be taking pictures. The bear was coming nearer and nearer, and I took no comfort from the thought of greeting him from a prone position. Perhaps he had not yet noticed this strange creature blocking his path? I decided to show myself clearly. That would stop him—or at least give him pause for thought. I stood up. The male continued as if I were just another one of the fuel drums.

I suddenly realized that my hard-won feeling of superiority was evaporating more quickly than I would have expected only a few short minutes ago. I had to keep on top of the situation. I decided that I would have an easier time establishing my dominance if I were nearer the cabin—especially as I had no shovel this time, only the camera. Trying to preserve my dignity, I walked slowly toward the cabin. The male gave no sign he had noticed me. In fact, the way he totally ignored me was somehow offensive.

I reached the porch, where Tolya and Hugh stood watching, and waited to see what would happen next. Thirty feet (10 m) from the blind, the bear turned to the cabin. It was time for me to put on a display. I grabbed the shovel and took a few aggressive steps toward the bear. Once again he totally ignored me. He was approaching the porch as inevitably as polar night comes to the Arctic each autumn. It was obvious that my method was not working. I would have gotten more of a reaction from a brick wall.

At a loss, I retreated to the porch. Suddenly, the male reacted, but not in the way I had been expecting. He looked at me at last and immediately, without hesitation, walked straight toward me. He showed no signs of aggression, no fear, no excitement, no emotions at all. He behaved like a giant who has noticed an insect in his path and has decided to take a closer look. He was definitely not like the other bears.

When he was no more than fifteen feet (5 m) away, I threw a rock at him and hit him on the hip. The great beast started, turned his head back sharply, and looked puzzled. There was nobody behind him. Then, he turned his head back to the porch with a look of mild surprise. He took two more steps forward. I threw another rock, which grazed his shoulder. And then this giant once again behaved in a manner I had completely failed to anticipate—he suddenly got terribly frightened.

The bear's massive body recoiled. He turned away sharply, and, as unhesitatingly as he had approached, he ran back to the coastal ridge. Maybe he had finally realized that those dark creatures in his way were human beings, which are always dangerous. Either that, or when I hit him with the rocks, he got disoriented, not knowing where the unseen danger was coming from. Anyway, he left, leaving the battleground to me.

By the time the bear was beating his retreat, the walruses on the beach in front of the cabin had formed a wall of bodies between the coastal ridge and the sea. The male jumped down the small cliff to the beach and ran at the walruses so quickly that they did not even have time to part to let him pass. Without stopping, the male rushed toward the walruses and started forcing his way through the mass of bodies. He did not bite them. He did not try to seize them. He just wanted to be safely in the sea. But the walruses could not understand that, and they began to panic. Pushing each other and splashing into the water, they, too, rushed to escape. One large female hit the bear's shoulder hard with her tusks. He jumped but did not even turn his head. He just kept going. In a few seconds, the bear and most of the walruses were out beyond the surf. The bear had to weave his way between the walruses to reach open water. As soon as he did, he disappeared beneath the waves. The second male made a run for it as soon as he saw people. He had no need to break through the walruses on the beach; the great male had already opened the wall for him.

Once again I had won, but I did not feel any satisfaction. I just could not understand this bear. I had to find a convincing explanation for his actions, a key to his mind. When I talked about him with the others, I called him "Grandfather," and this became his name. "All

Grandfather, Cape Blossom
The bear I called Grandfather seemed to rule the spit. He walked slowly along the beach with a regal presence, paying little attention to the walruses. The walruses, however, recognized the power and potential danger in Grandfather's heavy step, and at his approach, all escaped into sea.

Grandfather attacks, Cape Blossom
At the moment my camera shutter clicked, Grandfather interrupted his meal and rushed to attack me. I was not at all prepared for such a turn of events.

The moment the camera shutter clicked, Grandfather rushed to attack me.

right," I told myself, "Take it easy. It's no big deal. He is just an old guy who thinks slowly and doesn't see too well. He simply couldn't make out what I was at a distance. His speedy retreat shows he is afraid of people like all the other bears. I'll be able to manage him now that I have established my dominance."

I did not have to wait long to check out my interpretation of our encounter. Meanwhile, perhaps he had been developing a theory of his own.

~

The next day at noon, Grandfather appeared from the eastern side of the cabin. This time, there were no walruses on the beach. On his way to the cabin, Grandfather passed a mature female with two cubs, walking in the opposite direction. As they crossed paths fifty feet (15 m) from each other, the female lowered her head to show her respect for Grandfather but also to show her readiness to defend her children. Grandfather smelled her and went on his way. Eighty feet (25 m) from the cabin, he found the skin of a freshly killed walrus calf, investigated it, and started to feed.

Fifty feet (15 m) from the skin, right between the bear and the cabin, there were three old fuel drums full of garbage. I decided to take a picture of Grandfather from behind this shelter. I grabbed my camera, got to the fuel drums, and aimed the lens at the bear. The moment the shutter clicked, Grandfather rushed to attack me. Once again I was unprepared for his reaction. After yesterday's win, I had been confident that my dominance over him had been established forever, and that he would respect me and avoid me under any circumstances. So much for that idea.

I had no time to ponder the situation. I dashed up to the cabin thinking I might grab a stone or a stick on my way. I had started out only forty feet (12 m) from the porch. As I took my third step, I stumbled over a wire. I took two more steps as I struggled in vain to keep my balance. Finally I dropped down onto my knees. Trying to save the camera while I fell, I pushed it up sharply and hit myself on the nose. The camera was heavy—it was a Nikon F3 with a motor drive and a 300-millimeter lens—and for a moment I was blinded by pain. When I could think again, I realized that my stumbling flight had not improved my situation. I was on my knees, with blood pouring from my nose, unable to move, with no stick or stone at hand—but I was carefully cradling the camera. I could not imagine a more stupid position from which to confront a mature male polar bear on the attack. Where was the bear anyway? I wondered. Why wasn't he mixing me up in a mass of bloody flesh and bones? I turned my head slowly to the left, where I had last seen him before I fell. I was amazed and relieved to see that he was not pressing his advantage. From twenty feet (7 m) away he was looking at me with slight surprise, as if he was wondering what on earth I was doing down there.

Overcome with pain, I got up and made it to the porch. Grandfather moved forward as well, watching me with a puzzled expression on his face and smelling the air. We reached the level of the cabin simultaneously, but he was still fifteen feet (5 m) to my right. Grandfather stopped, took a few steps to the left, and then, at last, he caught the strong smell of human on the wind. Grandfather reacted as if the smell had hit him in the face. He jumped back, squatted down a little, and looked straight at the humans at the doorway. Then he turned and ran quickly to the spit and into the water. Three hundred feet (100 m) or so from the shore, he calmed down and turned back. When he reached the beach, he got out of the water and walked slowly to the top of the spit. Once again I was a winner—on the strength of my smell.

This triumph did not do much for my self-esteem either. Thinking the situation over from the scientific point of view, I decided that the incident did give me a key to Grandfather's behavior. I concluded that he was seriously afraid of my smell. I decided that the reason he had been unaware of me for such a long time on our first meeting was because the wind was blowing my smell away from him. From now on, I would keep him downwind.

~

After that, I did not see Grandfather for a couple of days. The third time we met was on September 19. The weather was good, and Tolya accompanied me to the end of the peninsula, where we spent the day observing bears and walruses from the top of the tower. The bears on the spit were active that day, and we were busy all day long recording our observations. The fresh wind from the sea and long hours of

Siberian lemming, Wrangel Island
A Siberian lemming emerges from of its den on a calm autumn day, wary of any hungry Arctic fox on patrol nearby. A Siberian lemming and hoofed lemming subspecies that appear only on Wrangel Island are separate species from their relatives on the Siberian mainland. Lemmings inhabit the coastal tundra and are common prey of the Arctic fox. When the ocean starts to freeze and the lemmings go underground, the fox move to the ice to find other food.

watching made us feel extremely hungry and a little cold. At about six in the evening, we came down the ladder and walked back to the cabin.

Igor, who was observing the beach from the roof of the cabin, later told us that about thirty minutes before we started back, Grandfather had appeared from the spit and had walked along the beach in the direction of the cabin. About a third of a mile (0.5 km) away, he sat down on the beach and quietly contemplated the sea for twenty minutes or so. Then he stood up and walked slowly up to the cabin. At the edge of the camp, where the tundra lowers itself down to the spit, he sniffed the gravel, made a day bed, and laid down, just behind the stack of fuel drums. From here he had a clear view of our approach.

At first our walk home was easy. A few bears were in our way as we started out, but they cleared off as soon as they saw us moving. As we walked along the spit, we discussed our day and forgot about bears for a while. One mature male was walking in the same direction we were, about a third of a mile (0.5 km) in front of us. Igor told us later that it was a bear we had called "Big Serpent." Big Serpent came up to Grandfather, and they sniffed each other's noses. Then Big Serpent lay down fifty feet (15 m) from Grandfather on the other side of the stack of fuel drums. From a distance, the two bears looked like a couple of pieces of white camp gear. The wind was from the northeast, and we were downwind of them. I was 300 feet (100 m) away when I realized that the white shape by the barrels was Grandfather. What other bear would rest right on the campground?

We altered our route to avoid Grandfather and to get him downwind as soon as we could. When we were 130 feet (40 m) from him, he got up and walked slowly to meet us. I could clearly see his disdainful grin. Grandfather was going to cut us off before we could give him a chance to catch our scent. We all got a strong urge to speed up, but we forced ourselves to look nonchalant. Grandfather would have plenty of time to meet us before we could escape, should he wish to do so; however, he held back and deliberately let us pass.

I felt more confident as we reached the slope leading up to the cabin. We made a loop around Grandfather. He could not escape from our smell now, and we had the added advantage of the high ground. Once again he surprised me. He did not get frightened; he did not run away. He just stood there sixty feet (20 m) away, smelling the air. For a couple of minutes, bear and humans looked at each other. Then the bear turned and walked slowly away without looking back. I took off my rucksack and rushed forward a few yards, as if chasing him. He did not even turn his head. He had no wish to stay near us, but he also did not want to run away. He was leaving with dignity. As soon as Big Serpent saw us, he made off in the opposite direction. So once again, I

Arctic fox, Wrangel Island

Arctic fox, as well as several other wildlife species including marine mammals and birds, winter in or near the Wrangel polynyas, the open areas amid the sea ice. Scavenging along the edges of the ice or following polar bear tracks, the fox often have luck finding carcasses of dead wildlife or the remains of bear kills that then become their sustenance. The Arctic fox also hunt seal cubs.

had failed to predict what Grandfather would do.

As I followed Grandfather with my eyes, I thought there was something symbolic about his lonely figure moving away against sunset. The big mature male polar bear, a dominant figure in polar bear society, had been pushed from his territory by a much weaker animal. Human beings have forced the giant bear to the very end of the spit, to the last point where, among the accumulated bones of walruses dead from natural causes or killed by hunters, his folk are now surrounded by the stormy sea. I felt ashamed that we humans are leaving animals no place on planet Earth, even though it belongs to them as much as it belongs to us. On this beautiful evening, I was surrounded by wonderful Arctic wilderness, yet I could not shake this feeling of melancholy and guilt.

∿

After that interaction, I did not meet Grandfather again at close quarters; however, there was one more episode that involved him. One morning later in October when Igor was trying to leave the cabin, he could not open the door. It was blocked from the outside by a polar bear resting against it. It was Grandfather, of course. He relinquished his spot on the porch only after Igor pushed the door against him several times with all his strength.

What was Grandfather trying to prove? Was it another demonstration of his rights to the territory? I did not know.

Blue Arctic fox, Wrangel Island
The blue Arctic fox is a rare dark-furred form of the species, occurring with an average frequency of one blue fox per thousand whites. Alongside his white relatives, this young blue fox appears misplaced, like a stranger to the Arctic's white world.

Chapter 4

The Great Walrus Hunt

For a long time the relationship between polar bears and walruses remained a mystery even for scientists who specialized in the study of Arctic marine mammals. The human imagination easily filled the gap in knowledge. There are numerous myths told by Native peoples about how the giant polar bear can kill a mature walrus with one blow of its powerful paw, or how the massive walrus can drown a mature polar bear by pulling it under water with its tusks.

Polar bears and walruses live in a harsh environment far from human settlement, so it is difficult to gather information on their relationship. Before I started my observations on Wrangel, a few scattered records reported the discovery of walrus carcasses surrounded by the tracks of polar bears; however, the evidence did not shed much light on how the walruses had died. In a couple of scientific papers, Russian researchers reported observing polar bears approaching small walrus rookeries and the walruses escaping in the sea. An extensive nine-year study in the Canadian High Arctic by Dr. Ian Stirling and his colleagues at the Canadian Wildlife Service turned up only ten cases of walruses possibly killed and certainly consumed by polar bears. In addition to these ambiguous results, the studies had been conducted in winter and early spring and, therefore, did not address important questions about the role of walruses in the diet of polar bears in the late spring, summer, and autumn seasons, when the bears are laying down reserves of fat in preparation for the winter. There was still much we did not know.

Walrus hunt, Cape Blossom
While the walruses were enjoying a calm, sunny autumn day hauled out on the gravel of the spit, this hungry male polar bear jumped down onto the beach from the tundra break and rushed to attack the rookery. The startled walruses rushed back into the sea like a massive wave rolling back off of the shore.

Walrus, Cape Blossom

Walruses prefer to haul out on ice floes where they are safer from bears. While resting on the floes, however, walruses always keep a watch on the conditions of the moving ice to avoid being locked in by compressed ice fields. Their long tusks serve at times as an anchor to hold them on the ice floe. In the absence of ice, walruses form rookeries on shore, but always keep a look out for preying white bears so they have plenty of time to escape back into the sea.

In my four years observing polar bears and walruses on Wrangel Island in the spring and autumn, I witnessed a total of thirty-five hunting events in which polar bears approached and attempted to seize walruses. The number of interactions correlated with the number of walruses and their hauling-out activity, which, in turn, related to the ice conditions of the season. In 1990, there were up to 60,000 walruses around Cape Blossom, of which 10,000 could be on the beach at any one time. In 1991, there were 2,500 walruses, with up to 300 on the beach. No walruses came to Cape Blossom in 1992, but in 1993 there were 3,000, with up to 500 on the beach. Most of the hunting events I observed occurred in 1990—twenty-five attempts—with four in 1991, none in 1992, and six in 1993.

Some hunts I could not watch from beginning to end, and many I did not see at all: If they took place out of the observation area or too early in the morning or too late in the evening, all I got to see were satiated polar bears. In these cases, I had no way of knowing whether the bears had killed the walruses they had consumed or whether they had died and been washed up on the beach.

I do know from my observations that to kill a walrus is not an easy task even for a mature polar bear. I observed only two successful attempts by polar bears to hunt walruses on land, and in both cases walrus calves were killed. Both successful hunts took place in 1990 and represent 8 percent of all attempted hunts on land that I observed that season. Over the course of the eight seasons I observed the bears, the success rate dropped to 5.7 percent.

The total number of walruses harvested by polar bears in 1990 was more impressive. During and after the hunting season, we found a total of fifty-five walrus carcasses on the southern and southwestern coasts of Wrangel Island. All but two of these were found around two major rookeries—one at Cape Blossom and the other at Doubtful Spit. Although bears consumed all these walruses, they certainly did not kill all of them. Some were washed ashore already dead; others may have been crushed to death on the beach by panicked relatives. At Cape Blossom, 63 percent of walruses eaten by polar bears in 1990 were calves born that year. Nursing calves from one to three years old were the next most vulnerable category, representing 27 percent of the carcasses. Only 10 percent of the dead walruses were mature animals. Despite earlier opinions that polar bears do not actively pursue walruses, I now knew without a doubt that polar bears hunt walruses to eat; I hunted the bears to learn how it was done.

～

A polar bear hunting a walrus is a most impressive—and most difficult—event to observe. Because we could never predict when or where the next hunt would take place, we had to wait long hours in the cold, exposed to the wind and wet snow. Some days there were just no walruses around. Stormy weather might keep them away from the beach for days at a time. When the cold autumn winds subsided, however, the exhausted walruses hurried to haul out to rest on solid ground. The hungry bears were waiting.

On September 16, 1990, the sea on the west side of Cape Blossom was rough, and tens of thousands of walruses were concentrated along the southern beach in a strip three miles (5 km) long. The rookery was nervous. Walruses were moving all the time, with new wedges forming here and there, spreading over, merging together, and moving back into the sea when troubled by an approaching bear—or for no apparent reason. They reminded me of waves: All day long they rolled onto and over the beach and streamed away again in a continuous fluid motion. The walruses just could not relax with that many bears around.

After waiting out the stormy weather on their day beds, the polar bears were restless, too. As the walruses hauled out, the bears patrolled the coast. The mature ones were on the lookout for likely victims; the weaker, more inexperienced bears were on the lookout for kills already made by the hunters.

I was on the edge of the coastal ridge viewing a new wedge of the rookery only 250 feet (80 m) from our porch, when a skinny adult bear appeared from around the cabin, ran to the edge of the small cliff, and jumped down onto the beach. He was so intent on the walruses that he did not even glance at me, even though as I was in full view. He could

Male bear stalking walrus, Cape Blossom
Once they get on shore, polar bears follow the coastline until they find a food source such as a walrus rookery or a wedge of ice on which to hunt seals. Females bears with cubs and young bears sometimes go inland, but mature bears like this one always prefer to stay close to the sea. This male caught a scent of the coastal walrus rookery and is heading directly to Cape Blossom.

A polar bear hunting a walrus is a most impressive thing to observe.

Bear and walrus confronted each other. The male bear tried to get to the walrus cow, but when he moved forward, she lunged at him with her tusks, striking the gravel right in front of his nose. Each time her defensive thrusts stopped the bear.

not see the walruses from the tundra and had obviously become excited when he heard their loud barks. On the beach, he hurried toward the walruses, who in turn hurried toward the sea.

The bear stopped right in front of the rearguard of the rookery, which had not had time to escape. These were mature walruses that had led the others onto the beach. First onto the beach, they now found themselves at the back of the line to return to the water. They aimed their tusks in the direction of the approaching bear. The bear hesitated a moment, then rushed to the attack. His chosen victim, a large female, was just about to dive into the surf. She lunged at the bear with her tusks, then turned and made a dash for the water. The bear tried to stop her by biting her back and grabbing her hind flippers, but he could not pierce the walrus's thick skin. She literally dragged the bear along as she made for the sea. The bear was no match for her bulk and power and soon gave up.

By this time, there was only one walrus left on the beach. Bear and walrus confronted each other for a couple of minutes, with the bear five feet (1.5 m) from the walrus. He tried to get to her, but when he moved forward, she lunged at him with her tusks, striking the gravel right in front of his nose. Each time her defensive thrusts stopped the bear. The bear gave up and decided to try his luck in the water instead.

He followed the swimming walruses for a while before returning to the female on the beach. She was lying at the edge of the beach leaning her head on her tusks, which were stuck in the gravel. She was obviously too exhausted to move. The bear approached from one side, then from the other. He even went into the water, intending to come up on her from behind. Every time she stopped his advances by lunging at him with her tusks. One time, he was so close she grazed his leg.

At last, moving slowly backward, she reached the sea and disappeared beneath the waves. The bear looked disappointed. He tried his luck in the water one more time, but was chased off by an aggressive walrus. The hunt was over. Back on land, the disgruntled bear paced along the beach, forcing any walruses resting there back into the sea. In four minutes he had cleared the beach. Having recovered some of his dignity, he disappeared over the top of the spit.

Bears of both sexes and all ages were excited about walruses, but I noticed great differences in their attitudes, hunting initiatives, and skills. Younger bears were always interested but tentative. They were not yet capable of hunting these giants. When there was no ice and these young bears were stuck on the beach, they were completely dependent on walrus remains left by mature bears. From what I observed, the mature females seem to be more prudent hunters than the males.

That same day in 1990, a well-fed female demonstrated her hunting skills. She appeared along the coastal ridge from the east. When she was 230 feet (70 m) from the walruses hauling out onto the beach near

Polar bear attack, Cape Blossom
Appearing suddenly over the beach break, a mature male polar bear charges a walrus rookery. While the majority of the walruses rush to the sea, an exhausted mature female walrus in front of the main rookery was directly in the path of the attacking bear. Seizing this lone walrus, the bear tried to hold her down from behind with his weight while clasping her massive body with his forepaws. The bear bit the walrus's back, neck, and head—even rode on her back—but the walrus eventually escaped into the sea. Still determined, the bear rushed to attack the main rookery, running along the front, trying to penetrate the mass of walruses to find a calf. Packed in close to each other, the walruses formed a wall with their bodies, which, combined with the use of their tusks for fighting, served as an effective defense against the attack. This polar bear went away still hungry.

Walrus hunt, Cape Blossom

A male polar bear charges a rookery of walrus, but most of them rush back into the sea before the bear could seize them. One mature female decided to do otherwise; she turned to confront the bear with her long tusks. Stymied by the daunting tusks aimed at his face, the bear paused, looking for a way to outflank the walrus's defenses. Facing the bear and ready to strike, the walrus slowly moved backward to escape into the sea. All the unlucky hunter could do was watch his lost prey swim away.

the cabin, she jumped down the small cliff and ran quickly along the front of the rookery, creating panic among the animals, all the while scanning the mass as if searching for something. Suddenly she rushed toward one group of fleeing walruses, mixed in with the rearguard for a moment, and snatched out a small calf. It was a calf-of-the-year, and its mother had obviously lost sight of it in the crush.

The bear pulled the calf away from the adult walruses and threw it sharply aside. Then, she caught the calf by its neck and repeated the process. All the walruses left, except the calf's mother, who looked to be no more than seven to ten years old. She hung around the edge of the beach, looking on as the bear bit her calf, but it was too late for her to defend her baby.

The bear was just starting to tear the skin off the calf's head, holding its body with her paw, when, all of a sudden, a larger bear appeared on the scene. It was a mature male. He jumped down to the beach and hurried toward the female and her prey. The female looked up and made a sharp dash to the side to indicate that the carcass belonged to her. The male was not impressed. He quickly approached, seized the calf, and pushed the female in the chest with his paw. The female abandoned her prey without a fight. The male bear grabbed the stolen carcass in his teeth and hauled it up the ridge and out onto the tundra. There he lay down on it, completely covering the dead calf with his massive body. Alone with his meal, he started chewing a hole in the skin.

Meanwhile, the robbed female went back to hunting to make up for her loss. She ran along the beach toward the next wedge of the forming rookery and repeated the same hunting procedure. When she was eighty feet (25 m) from the walruses, they turned for the water. In the ensuing panic, she made a short rush to the left and seized another small calf. It all happened so quickly that no walrus even tried to defend it.

This time the female took precautions to safeguard her prey from would-be robbers. She pulled the calf to the base of the spit, bit it several times in the head, then pulled it across the spit to the lagoon. There she entered the sea and sank the calf, which was still alive, in the water a few yards from the beach. Then, holding the carcass down with her paw, she looked around to make sure no bears were chasing her. This time she was determined nobody was going to steal her prey and she kept the carcass under water as she tore it apart. The sea was soon stained red with blood. After five minutes or so, she obviously decided it was too difficult to tear the calf apart under water, and she pulled the carcass onto the beach, where she continued her meal. For about half an hour she dined alone. Then, one by one, some young bears joined the meal and after an hour, four bears were gorging themselves on the remains. About that time, the satiated hunter left.

The mature male bears I have observed seemed to employ riskier methods of hunting than the females. I have frequently seen them attacking adult walruses and initiating direct physical contact with these well-armed giants. In 1990, I observed at least four cases when male polar bears were injured while attacking mature walruses. I noticed another five males wandering around with bloody wounds inflicted by walrus tusks. In a way, risky hunting ventures make sense: Day after day we watched the same increasingly exhausted walrus on the beach, its thick skin crossed with deep wounds from attacking bears. It is quite possible that a walrus that is repeatedly attacked and wounded is well on its way to an early demise, thus increasing the polar bears' chances of getting a meal. So the hunter who takes risks is actually working to feed the whole polar bear community.

It also became clear to me that hunting walruses is an inherently risky business for polar bears. From the groups I observed, only a few experienced animals were able to make a kill, and the walruses killed were all calves. No single bear is capable of stopping a mature walrus by holding onto its hind flippers or—another technique I observed—by grabbing it with its forelegs while biting its back and head. As long as the adult walrus can reach the sea, it will escape. Most bears were forced to feed on the remains of another bear's kill or to scavenge old dry skins of walruses that had died in previous years. In 1990, we came across four bears that had died of starvation.

Hunting walruses is an inherently risky business for polar bears. No single bear is capable of stopping a mature walrus by holding onto its hind flippers or by grabbing it with its forelegs while biting its back and head.

One of the most exciting hunts I witnessed happened about a week after we had started filming in 1990. After a severe storm that lasted three days, exhausted walruses started hauling out onto the beach. Undisturbed by bears, the rookery had been forming since early morning. By noon it came to within 250 feet (80 m) of where Hugh and I were hiding behind a row of empty fuel drums on the edge of the coastal ridge. After three hours of watching the rookery, Hugh suddenly touched my shoulder. "There's a bear coming from the other side. Should we move to the cabin and let him pass?" I looked back, but there was no time for us to move without him spotting us—something that might disturb him and ruin his hunt. "We have to stay put. Let him pass us and see what happens," I whispered.

The bear was stepping widely, pushing his paws out to the side, keeping his head horizontal and moving it slightly from side to side as he walked. His eyes were screwed up a little. He was walking straight toward our shelter. We froze. The bear was obviously hungry, and the walruses had his undivided attention. As he approached the edge of the tundra, he speeded up, aiming his nose, eyes, and ears at the walruses. He passed us on the other side of the fuel drums, no more than three feet (1 m) away from me. I could clearly see every hair on his body, and I could easily have reached out to touch him. So intent was he on the walruses that he did not even notice us. Only once did he turn his

Feasting bear, Cape Blossom
After a female polar bear successfully killed a walrus calf, this male bear stole her prey. He dragged the calf up onto the tundra and started tearing open the carcass; it took forty minutes for him to break through the calf's dense skin. To protect his dinner from possible competitors, the bear lay down on it to cover the carcass as he ate. When he spotted me taking photos, he raised himself up above the prey to display his rights to the carcass. After he had gorged himself on the calf, he left the remains to two waiting young bears and strolled into the surf to wash off the fat and blood that stained his fur.

Bears in a walrus "bone field," Cape Blossom

When the polar bears were unlucky in their walrus hunting, they fed on old walrus carcasses from a field of bones and remains of old kills. The "herd" of polar bears "grazing" on the old walrus skins reminded me of a herd of cows grazing in a meadow.

head slightly to the left and glance toward the cabin. I wondered later what would have happened had he glanced to the right and realized we were so close. When he was sixty feet (20 m) beyond our hiding place, he jumped down onto the beach and ran toward the walruses. We switched on our cameras.

An ancient female walrus, perhaps fifteen years old or more, was lying with her head on the gravel some distance from the main rookery. She was not much more than a grayish-brown bag of skin and bones, and looked more dead than alive. As she did not react to the approaching bear, he switched from running to walking. When he touched her, first with his nose and teeth and then, when she moved, with his paw, she surprised him by making a lunge with her tusks and turning for the sea. The bear was getting more than he had bargained for. He started to bite her and tried to hold onto her with his paws. He even rode on her back. But she was moving forward like a tank. The bear bit her back, her neck, and her head, but he could not stop her. Despite her emaciated state, she was still massive and enormously powerful. She escaped, and the male turned his attentions to the main rookery.

It was not his lucky day. There were many walruses on the beach, but the ones at the front of the rookery were all mature adults, and the bear could not break through their ranks to get at the calves within. He attacked again and again, first at one place and then at another. Each time he was confronted by walruses who lunged at him with their tusks. One time a blow to his chest drew blood. Another time he jumped right into the mass of bodies and disappeared from view. Perhaps he was aiming for a calf. A few seconds later he reappeared with no prey but with bloody scratches on his face.

Unlike the female we had observed earlier, who had kept to the edge of the rookery, this male was trying to break right into it. I could not help thinking that if he had applied the female's tactics he might have had better luck.

Luck, in many ways, is what it is all about. Hunting large prey is a gamble in which the stakes are high—life or death—and the odds of winning are evenly split between hunter and prey. Predators in the wild have to work hard and take risks in order to get their meals. They are not like human hunters, who sit in comfortable shelters and use modern rifles, risking nothing and with little riding on the hunt. I followed the male with my eyes as long as I could. Sometimes, clouds of snow hid him from my view. He was still running along the rookery, leaving some walruses on the beach behind him, when, turning around the corner, he finally disappeared.

Maybe he made his lucky lunge later that day, but I would never know. A cold wind was blowing, but I remained motionless: In my mind I was running along the rookery with him.

Luck is what it is all about. Hunting large prey is a gamble in which the stakes are high—life or death—and the odds of winning are split between hunter and prey. Predators in the wild have to take risks in order to get their meals.

69

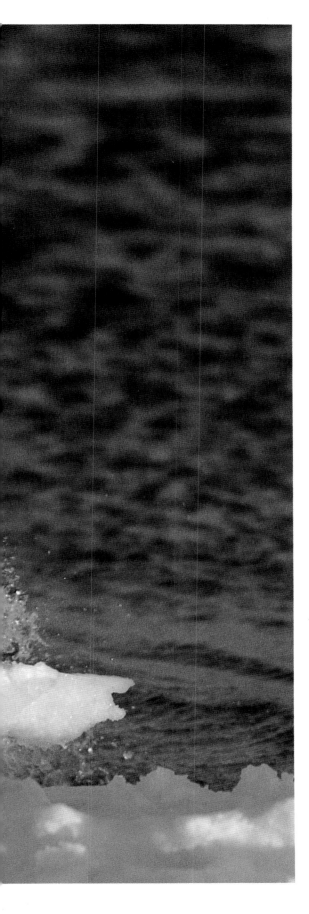

Chapter 5

Giants at Sea

There is a belief, not only among indigenous people of Chukotka, that when a walrus meets a swimming polar bear, it takes its revenge and kills the enemy. Might that be true? Walruses are social marine mammals. They defend their relatives and, when hunted by people, often get aggressive and attack boats. Polar bears are good swimmers but cannot compare to walruses in this skill. In the sea, polar bears could be easy victims for these well-armed divers, should they wish to take revenge for being hunted on solid ground. With such a high concentration of walruses in the water at Cape Blossom in the autumn of 1990, I had a good opportunity to check these attitudes and to investigate how the drama that starts on the beach continues in the sea.

The day after our arrival in 1990, Hugh and I were taking a short walk when we noticed a young male bear on the beach. He was examining the carcass of an adult walrus that was rolling in the surf. A second young male in the tundra was walking along parallel to the coast. The moment the second bear noticed us, he took fright and ran toward the coastal ridge. When he reached it, the first bear saw him hurriedly approaching and took fright as well. He abandoned the carcass, entered the water, and swam away. The second bear followed the first. So there they were swimming away—the first bear looking suspiciously back at the second bear, who in turn was looking back at us. None of the walruses that were swimming in the vicinity approached the bears.

Emerging from the sea, Wrangel Island
While polar bears are equally at home on land and ice, they are also marine animals and readily plunge into the icy sea to cross open water or to hunt. The white bears are good swimmers, able to swim long distances of perhaps some tens of miles up to even a hundred miles—their swimming limit is not known.

This somewhat comical scene was typical of the interactions we saw every day at Cape Blossom. When polar bears entered the water, which they seemed to do without hesitation when walruses were around, the walruses tended to keep their distance. If a walrus happened to find itself in the way of a swimming polar bear, it always dove beneath the waves or swam faster to leave the area. At the same time, walruses in the sea were obviously more confident around polar bears than they were on land. Occasionally they came within ten feet or so (a few meters) of swimming bears before diving beneath the waves. So, my first impression was that in the water each side seemed to more or less leave the other side alone. Further observations, however, forced me to change this simplistic analysis.

In nature, sometimes what does not happen can be even more revealing than what does. For instance, an animal may not do something, not because it does not want or need to, but because there is a strong reason for not doing it. To make sense of such indirect evidence, you have to know your subject well. My observation of the attitude of polar bears toward walruses in the sea is a case in point. Only after the 1991 season, when there were fewer walruses at Cape Blossom, did I realize that in 1990, although we did see a lot of bears in the water, there were not as many swimming bears as one might have expected. As I result of my later observations, I began to understand that polar bears are not comfortable entering the water when there are a lot of walruses around. Since there were more walruses in 1990, I observed more interactions between polar bears and walruses on the beach than in the water; in 1991, the proportion was reversed.

In 1991, the walruses congregated at the end of the spit, which was also where the polar bears liked to be. There were significantly fewer bears than in 1990, and they were more sensitive to my presence. In 1990, I had been able to walk among the bears without causing them too much consternation, but in 1991, every visit to the spit was like a game of chess. I had to pick my moves carefully so as to disturb as few animals as possible. I could not, however, avoid causing at least a few of them to seek refuge in the water.

On the evening of September 19, 1991, I was sitting on the platform at the top of the reflector tower, thinking about the evening meal and the warm stove in the cabin when, at about five in the afternoon, a mature male polar bear at the end of the spit stood up on his hind legs to smell the air. At the same moment, a subadult who was wandering just beneath the tower caught my scent. The young bear took fright and ran quickly to the top of the spit. The male bear, who certainly could not smell me from where he was standing, watched the

Swimming between ice floes, Chukchi Sea

An adult bear swims between ice floes. When troubled on land, polar bears often escape onto the ice or into the water, proving that they are true marine animals.

In nature, sometimes what does not happen can be even more revealing than what does. An animal may not do something, not because it does not want or need to, but because there is a strong reason for not doing it.

Walruses and swimming bears, Wrangel Island

A male and female bear pass a herd of walruses while swimming off Wrangel. Myths and legends told by the Chukotka people tell of walruses taking revenge on polar bears for attacking them while on land by drowning the bears in the water. I observed polar bears fearlessly swimming among walruses, with no risk to themselves. In my research, I saw swimming walruses who found themselves too close to a polar bear, or walruses who surfaced near a bear; these walruses would simply dive and swim

Above: Swimming bear, Chukchi Sea
At all times of the year, polar bears often have to swim to cross the leads and polynyas during their daily rounds or while hunting seals. During seasons when local ice fields melt and the edge of Arctic pack ice moves too far to the north from Wrangel, polar bears lose this solid "ground" in the sea and are forced to spend much of their time in the water.

Opposite: Shaking off water, Chukchi Sea
A polar bear shakes himself to get rid of water in his fur as he emerges from a swim in the icy sea.

Polar bears are cautious and even afraid of walruses while in the water.

---

running subadult for a couple of seconds, got worried, and hurriedly went down the beach to the water. In his path was a female with two cubs. As soon as she saw the male rapidly walking toward her, she gathered up her cubs. When the male passed them, they rushed to the water and swam away.

A herd of about 150 walruses swam not far off the end of the spit. The male bear, seeing the female's panic and not knowing where the danger was coming from, decided to escape into the water as well. Polar bears, like other social animals, usually keep close to each other when they sense danger. In this case, the male followed the female with her cubs, but she did not like this. She put herself in between her cubs and the male, and several times she turned on him. The walruses closed ranks as the bears approached, and both groups began to look a little nervous.

The female found herself caught between the walrus herd and the male bear. She looked from one to the other and then swam to the left to distance herself from both dangers. The male was not comfortable either. He seemed to have been looking to the female as another bear to follow to safety. When she turned away from him, he seemed unsure of himself. Finally, perhaps deciding that she was headed in the wrong direction, he left her alone and circled around the herd and out into the open sea.

The female kept her distance from the herd, and when she finally realized that the male was not chasing her, she returned to the beach with her cubs in tow. On the beach, the mother went to the gravel hills, where the bears preferred to rest, smelled the male's day bed, and settled down nearby to nurse her cubs, who were eager to get some milk after their tiring swim.

The more I observed, the more convinced I became that polar bears are cautious and even afraid of walruses while in the water. In September 1993, while I was on my way to my observation area at the top of the spit, I surprised a young female and a mature male who swam away together, even though the female was obviously nervous about having the male join her in the water. A herd of about twenty walruses blocked the bears' escape route. The walruses were resting in a vertical position about 650 feet (200 m) from the shore with their heads up and their tusks parallel to the water. The bears stopped 100 feet (30 m) from the group, circled around several times on the spot, and turned back to the beach together. When they landed, they were again downwind from me and repeated their flight, only this time they swam a little farther to the right and passed the group of walruses.

Wringing out water, Wrangel Island
A wet polar bear drags himself across the ice, using the icy surface to wring water out of his fur.

So why were the bears so cautious around walruses in the water? I never saw walruses attack bears in the water. In the sea, as on land, the groups of walruses I observed were afraid of bears, indicating that their natural relationship with polar bears is as prey; however, I did see individual walruses come quite close to bears in the water, and once I watched an interaction in which the walrus appeared to be the aggressor.

⁓

It happened on September 24, 1991. The day was stormy, and many walruses had found shelter from the hard surf in calm water on the southern side of the spit. A female polar bear with two cubs-of-the-year and two adult males had escaped into the sea after a subadult bear had created panic by running to the top of the spit. At first, all five white heads of the swimming bears were close together, but soon the group split up. The males continued to the west, where the waves were higher, while the female headed her cubs in the direction of the calm water on the southern side of the spit. There she encountered the walruses. Several times, single walruses and groups of up to seven animals passed the family of bears, but the walruses did not approach any closer than about thirty feet (10 m).

Hidden by the heavy surf, a group of twelve walruses was bobbing on the waves fifty feet (15 m) from the bear family. Only when both groups were on the crests of their respective waves could the mother bear see the group of walruses. The moment she became aware of them, she changed course, putting herself between her cubs and the walruses and keeping her cubs about five feet (1.5 m) in front of her. There were so many walruses taking shelter from the storm that no matter where they turned, the bears could not avoid meeting them. Single walruses and small groups looked at the bears and dove or swam away. The bears were treading water and looking nervously around.

The mother had finally decided to head the cubs out to the west, when suddenly a large walrus surfaced barely fifteen feet (5 m) in front of the family. As the mother first turned away and then thought better of it and turned back, the adult walrus swam rapidly toward the family and did a forward-rolling dive right in front of them, coming as close to the bears as the mother was from her cubs. I could not make out the sex of the walrus, but there was no mistaking that it was big and it was excited. The bears looked worried. The walrus repeated this display two more times, then dove and disappeared. Immediately after that, the mother headed her cubs to the northwest and left the area.

From this and other observations, I soon learned that female polar bears with cubs are particularly cautious with walruses in the water, and young mothers are positively afraid of them. Once in 1991, I watched a young mother bear with a cub-of-the-year on an ice floe 300 feet (100 m) from shore. Walruses were circling around intending to haul out on the floe. The mother bear was eager to swim to the beach to get away from them, but she was afraid to enter the water with so many walruses swimming around. She hesitated and threatened any walrus that passed too near the floe. I sat in the cold wind as I waited to see what she would do. After half an hour I could hardly move my frozen fingers. I was ready to give up, when, at last, she found a moment when there were no walruses in the vicinity, and she jumped into the sea. The worried cub jumped after her with widely spread legs. The pair made it safely to the beach, and I retired to the cabin to coax my frozen fingers back to life.

After two years on Cape Blossom, I had observed tens of interactions between these two giants of the Arctic, both on the beach and in the sea; however, many questions remain unanswered. Every autumn, when walruses congregated around Wrangel Island, I saw bears with bloody injuries that looked as though they had been inflicted by walrus tusks. How had the bears received these injuries? Did mothers with cubs have serious reason to be afraid of walruses in the sea? To what extent can walruses be a danger to bears in their native environment? Do walruses occasionally kill bears? Would the risk for bears be higher if more mature male walruses came to Wrangel? The Arctic is not fast in opening its secrets, and the Arctic wildlife researcher has to be patient. I had to return to Cape Blossom for another two years before I could find out more about the endless drama between the largest hunter and its giant prey.

The walrus swam rapidly toward the bear family and did a forward-rolling dive right in front of them. The walrus was big and it was excited. The bears looked worried.

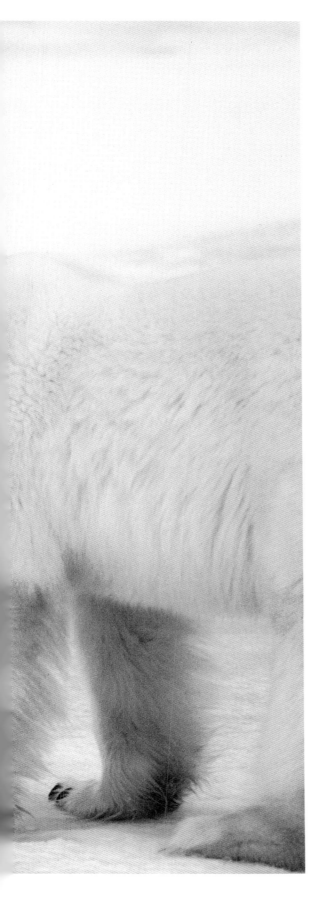

Chapter 6

The Social Ice Bear

In popular and scientific literature polar bears are reported to be solitary hunters. I did not doubt this statement when I came to Cape Blossom in 1990, so I was surprised to find nearly 150 bears within the observation area. It was hard to think of the polar bear as a solitary predator while observing a crowd of them on the end of the spit. To what extent then are they social creatures, and how do they react to one another at close quarters?

It is true that polar bears hunt alone. I never saw them cooperate to hunt a walrus, and if the polar bear's main prey is the ringed seal—a prey much smaller than the hunter—then there is no evolutionary need for polar bears to develop cooperative hunting skills. What I soon discovered, however, was that they do cooperate in consuming prey.

Playful bears
Polar bears are playful animals. Under favorable conditions in autumn, young and even adult bears may play together for hours.

Mother and cubs, Cape Blossom

Mother polar bears normally lead their cubs until the cubs are two and a half years old. Under their mother's protection, the cubs learn survival skills for the severe Arctic environment. The mother and her cubs are the basic social unit in the polar bear community, and even elder cubs will obey their mother implicitly in any serious situation, joining her to behave as a family unit. Some cubs, however, may be abandoned and turned out to live on their own in the second year. Such young would not be able to hunt successfully; they become hangers-on in the polar bear community, living on the remains of the adult bears' kills. This happens as a result of an accident, or when food resources are limited, and females can not support the family.

In 1990, we often observed more than one bear eating simultaneously from the same carcass. Four bears at a single walrus carcass was usual; occasionally we saw up to eight bears eating side by side; and once we found fourteen bears of both sexes and all ages around a dead walrus calf that had been washed up onto the beach. Usually, a hunter could not hide his success for long from the sensitive noses and watchful eyes of hangers-on. This, for instance, was the case with the female's successful hunt at Cape Blossom on September 16, 1990. The first to join her at her second kill was a subadult. I could not determine its sex, but it was more than likely a young female who was spending her first autumn without her mother. She approached the hunter with care, made a half circle around her, and gently bit the carcass, pulling it slightly toward her. Immediately, the older bear turned around and placed herself between the intruder and the meal. There was no aggression. The older bear simply blocked the younger one's access to the carcass.

The young female, however, did not give up. Begging was her only way to get food. Pressing herself against the ground, she moved in front of the hunter again. There she lay down with her head to the carcass, nosed forward, and nibbled on a piece of flesh. This time the older bear did not object. Good manners had won the day. For a few seconds they ate together, then the older bear left the carcass to get a drink from the lagoon. When she returned, the two bears continued to feed off opposite sides of the carcass. This time, the young bear tore harder on the flesh. Evidently, she now felt it was within her rights to do so. A couple of minutes later, they were joined by a couple of other young bears. When I left them, the four bears were eating peaceably together.

When several bears feed simultaneously from the same carcass, there can be a lot of growling and short open-mouthed lunges. This is normal behavior among pack mates and is typical of social predators such as wolves, hunting dogs, or lions; however, polar bears, who do not form packs, also tolerate each other around a kill. In fact, when eating from the same carcass, the polar bears I observed were more tolerant of each other than highly social wolf packs are around a kill. I soon realized that there was more to it than simple tolerance.

The bears I observed became "owners" of the carcass for the time they were feeding on it. Often the bear in possession of the carcass allowed other bears to join the feast and even left parts of the kill if another bear asked for them. I also observed a number of special behaviors used to solicit food: a slow gentle approach, a circle around the carcass, a nose-to-nose greeting with the bear in charge of the carcass. Although a bear usually did not leave the carcass for other bears until it finished its own meal, it did not try to assert its exclusive rights to the carcass.

One benefit of cooperative feeding is help in opening the carcass. Walrus skin is so thick that it takes a couple of hours for a polar bear to chew through it. This is why polar bears often open carcasses of adult walruses around the genitals where the skin is softer. Gradually the polar bears widen the hole. When they are finished eating, all that is left is the skin—which is often turned completely inside out—the backbone, and the skull. As the bears put their heads through the hole they have made to get at the fat and meat inside, they stain their fur with blood and, for some time after eating, walk around with bloody faces. After feeding, they clean their fur in the surf, where the waves act like the wash cycle of a washing machine.

～

On September 14, 1993, I watched a cooperative feeding effort. The previous day, an exhausted male walrus about six or seven years old had appeared on the southern beach at Cape Blossom. I noticed him in the evening on my way back from the spit. He was swimming slowly in the surf, looking for a place to haul out. A little later, I saw him on the beach about 650 feet (200 m) from the cabin. He lay on his side, his head flopped down on the gravel. For about ten minutes he lay still. Then he scooped up some gravel with his tusks to make a rough pillow for his head, but he could not seem to get comfortable. He repeated these digging efforts several times, then changed his position, hauling backward to the water a little, and flopped down again. Perhaps with little fat under his skin he found it painful to lie on the ground. It was obvious to me that he was dying but I had no idea why. Maybe he had been shot somewhere off the coast of the mainland? I could only guess. At dusk he left the beach for the water but hauled out again a half mile (1 km) farther from the cabin. The first thing I saw the next morning

Sharing prey, Cape Blossom
A group of mature males peacefully eat from the carcass of an adult walrus while a young mother with her cub-of-the-year waits for her turn to join the feast. Often as many as four to eight bears might join together at one walrus carcass, and on one occasion, fourteen bears were seen eating simultaneously, shoulder to shoulder. In congregations on the beach, polar bears show much higher social tolerance for fellow bears then on the ice.

Sharing prey, Cape Blossom
Unlucky in her walrus hunting, this mother with her two cubs-of-the-year satisfy themselves on the remains of a walrus calf taken by an adult male. As little meat is left on the bones by this time, the mother lets her cubs have the better pieces.

from the roof of the cabin was a group of bears with bloody faces gathered around his carcass.

I hurriedly finished my simple breakfast, grabbed my rucksack with my camera equipment and tape recorder, and walked to my observation point at the end of the spit. By the time I arrived, the feast was already far advanced; at least one-third of the carcass had been consumed. Two bloodstained males were thoroughly absorbed in the task at hand and were ignoring other bears that were eager for their turn. Another two mature males with bloody faces were resting on day beds 250 feet (80 m) away. They had already eaten their fill and needed time to digest before their next assault on the carcass.

One female bear was standing with her cub at the edge of a low gravel ridge fifteen feet (5 m) above the carcass nervously sniffing the meal. She was evidently afraid to lead her cub down but did not want to leave him behind while she went to the carcass alone. Another female with a cub was also holding back. Then one of the resting males decided to join the others at the carcass. He stopped about forty feet (12 m) away as if waiting in line. He was calm and even looked a little shy. This was too much for the first female. Here were two fat, ignorant males eating walrus fifteen feet (5 m) from her nose when she could not bring herself to join the feast, and now another guy with a bloody face was going to jump in line! She rushed to attack the waiting male, and her cub bravely followed, imitating her actions.

The male backed away, turned broadside, and bared his teeth. The female stopped about three feet (1 m) away from him, put her head down, and bared her teeth back at him. The other female decided to distance herself from the action. The first female retreated, then nervously renewed her attack. She did this three times, but each time the male stopped her by opening his mouth. On the fourth try, the second female unexpectedly joined in, and the male backed away, settling down some eighty feet (25 m) from the carcass. It was not clear which bear the second female intended to attack—the male or the first female—but the end result was positive for both female bears. They proceeded to ignore the male, and the braver of the two turned her attentions to the carcass.

Although the female was obviously nervous, the males at the carcass were so absorbed in their meal that they took little notice of her. She made several attempts to reach the carcass, but each time she turned back to her cub after a couple of steps. When at last she overcame her fear, the males made no objection to her joining them. They con-tinued happily chewing away while she ate for a couple of minutes on the other side with her head only five feet (1.5 m) from theirs. Her cub waited on the edge of the ridge fifteen feet (5 m) behind, and she often looked back at him. Once, the nervous female made a short lunge at one of the males. He just backed away slightly and continued chewing.

Soon, a subadult male approached. The cub made a short lunge at him as he passed the ridge, but the subadult just ignored him and headed straight for the carcass. First he settled down opposite the female, who lunged at him. He backed away a little but continued chewing. Then, perhaps looking for a tastier morsel, he decided to try the female's side of the carcass. He was now less than six feet (2 m) from her, and she made a quick open-mouthed lunge at him. Right then the second female decided to approach the carcass and passed too close to the cub of the first female. Immediately, the mother returned to her child and attacked the second female with her head low to the ground and her mouth open. The second mother mirrored the posture of the first, then retreated. The first female now decided she had had enough. She was extremely agitated and led her cub away. It was an hour before they returned.

In situations like this, with a high level of excitement and action, nuances of polar bear psychology can be quite pronounced. Many more such interactions can be observed when tens of polar bears gather around a great food source, such as a beached whale or a pile of dead walruses in a rookery. Large walrus rookeries inevitably leave some carcasses on the beach. Among the thousands of animals, there are always some in poor condition that will die sooner or later. Often if the animals panic, a few get crushed and die on the spot, or later, from internal injuries. Great catastrophes when tens or hundreds of walruses die at one time are not natural occurrences. However, when a rookery is disturbed by humans—as often happens at the coastal rookeries of Chukotka—a so-called anthropogenic panic occurs, causing immediate

The female bear put her head down and bared her teeth at the male bear. She retreated, then nervously renewed her attack. The male backed away.

mass death of walruses. During my seasons on Wrangel Island, I witnessed the aftermath of such a panic at a rookery on Doubtful Spit.

Doubtful Spit is right in the middle of the southern coast of Wrangel Island. It is a popular spot with walruses, and in September 1991, there were more walruses there than there were at Cape Blossom. Biologist Tolya Kochnev was observing them. The rookery on Doubtful Spit had started on September 19. By the next day, no fewer than 20,000 walruses were already hauled out onto the beach. It was a foggy day, and at about two o'clock in the afternoon, an ice-survey aircraft was fly-ing low over the coastline. The crew was lost and was looking for landmarks.

When the aircraft flew over the walrus rookery on Doubtful Spit, the pilot, of course, could not see what happened next. Thousands of walruses frightened by what was for them a terrifying noise, made for the sea at once. In their haste to reach the water, they clambered over each other until their bodies were stacked as many as four deep. This would be a terrible weight even for the strongest males to bear, and some animals were simply flattened. The aircraft found its way through the clouds leaving behind 104 dead walruses. Because of stormy weather, it was two days before observers could get to the spit. By that time, eight polar bears had already started work on the carcasses. The next day, eleven bears were reported. The situation developed rapidly.

On September 25, I interrupted my observations at Cape Blossom, collected my wife, Irina, who was observing migrating snowy owls at the cape, and drove the ATV to Doubtful Spit. For the next few days, Tolya and I investigated carcasses for a more precise understanding of the immediate cause of death—a task that would have been impossible for a single researcher—and watched polar bears at work amidst the unexpected bounty.

When I arrived, twenty-five polar bears were feasting. The dead walruses lay in a compact strip in the middle of the triangular end of the peninsula. At any time, fifteen to thirty bears of both sexes and all ages could be seen feeding on the carcasses. Bears that were not eating spent most of the time sleeping on their day beds, which were widely distributed over the spit. Dead walruses produce a strong smell, and the wind was sending promising messages to all sensitive noses for miles around. Every day brought new bears to the feeding ground. By the time I left on October 10 to continue my observations at Cape Blossom, there were fifty-six fat and happy polar bears at Doubtful Spit.

As I observed a kaleidoscope of activity on Doubtful Spit, I became increasingly impressed with the variety of polar bear characters and the seemingly endless possibilities for social interaction. One time, I watched a female and her cub abandon a carcass to a mature male even though the male had approached slowly and carefully showing no obvious signs of aggression. On another occasion, a mother and her cub stood shoulder to shoulder as they drove a mature male away from a carcass. Then there was the time I observed a massive male eating alongside a cub-of-the year while the mother stood patiently waiting

Dead walruses, Doubtful Spit

An airplane flew over Doubtful Spit on the south central coast of Wrangel on September 1991 at low altitude just above a large walrus rookery. In a panic, the walruses rushed into the sea, crushing 104 fellow walruses during their escape. Those near the water made it safely into the surf while others were simply flattened by the terrible weight of the giant, powerful animals in their frenzy. The dead walruses lay in a strip along the shore at the end of the spit.

for her child to finish. As I watched, I tried to make sense of what I saw. Which bears were allowed to eat in which order? How can social organization among polar bears be defined?

Once, in the autumn of 1993 at Cape Blossom, I observed one mature male politely solicit food from another. The first male, a really massive animal, was chewing on a dry, but still edible piece of walrus skin. A younger adult male approached and sniffed the air from about ten feet (a few meters) away. The older male noticed the younger one but did not react. The younger bear gently circled around a couple of times, getting gradually closer. Finally, he put his nose right up to the older bear's face and gently sniffed the walrus skin. The older bear turned his head to the younger one, and they touched noses. After the younger male had repeated this calming gesture two more times, the older one let him take the skin and slowly left the scene. The older male then went to the day-bed area, checking out other pieces of walrus skin on his way. The scene was a marked contrast to the other scene I observed that autumn when the two females were so nervous around the carcass on which the male bears were feeding.

~

So just how do groups of polar bears of different sexes react to one another? Even though mature males seemed tolerant of each other's company and even overtly friendly to one another, the females and young bears I observed usually preferred to give groups of mature males a wide berth. Only mature females did not seem to worry about

Feasting on walrus, Doubtful Spit
Polar bears of all sexes and ages take advantage of the walrus tragedy to gorge themselves on the piles of carcasses. Through evolution, the "solitary" polar bear has been instilled with well-developed mechanisms of tolerance towards its fellow bear; it is not unusual to observe tens of polar bears collecting at one spot around a rich food source, such as these walruses or a beached whale. All day long, until the carcasses were completely consumed, some twenty bears fed in turn on the walruses while a total of fifty to seventy polar bears were concentrated in the vicinity, sleeping between eating spells.

85

The polar bear family is a maternal social unit usually composed of a mother with her one, two, or three cubs.

passing close to a group of males. Perhaps their years of life experience allowed them to better estimate the level of risk involved. Although the mothers with cubs that I observed were intolerant, or at least suspicious, of adult males, they showed a high level of tolerance to each other. They seemed to realize that they belonged to the same social group and shared similar problems. Of course quarrels did erupt—usually when families mixed and the cub of one mother got too close to another, or while competing for food or for a popular spot for a day bed—however, such quarrels were rare events and short lived. The routine I observed between polar bear mothers was one of peaceful tolerance.

The polar bear family is a maternal social unit usually composed of a mother and her one, two, or three cubs. Sometimes, however, more complicated families can be found. I observed one such composite family on Doubtful Spit in September 1991 in the aftermath of the rookery disaster. There were four bears in this unit—a mother, her two year-old cubs, and a second adult female. This second female was obviously younger than the mother and a couple of years older than the cubs. Perhaps she was a cub from a previous breeding cycle. All four bears walked together, fed together, and slept in a pile in a single day bed.

Polar bear mothers normally raise their young to their third winter; however, some young bears are on their own by their second year. This percentage is different for different areas, depending on local environmental conditions and how the population as a whole is faring. Com-

Playful bears
Play among polar bears is believed to function as a way of learning about social hierarchy. While playing, however, it does not matter whether individual bears are younger or older, weaker or stronger; playing partners have equal rights. In addition, polar bears play so often simply because they enjoy it.

pared to young bears of the same age still under their mother's care, the lone subadults I observed were more flexible and adaptable in social situations; however, they also held a lower social position in the community. Every adult bear could easily push them away and nobody would defend them; even cubs under their mother's care dominated these subadults. Consequently, they had to be careful and wise in managing social distance. And they were indeed. Every autumn at Cape Blossom I observed subadult bears. They were always the hangers-on in the community, yet they were tolerated by the adults and allowed access to kills. I realized then that the high level of social tolerance among bears plays an important role in the survival of the entire population. For one thing, it helps such lone subadults survive until they are able to hunt and make their own contributions to the community.

The more I watched, the more I noticed that polar bears seem to enjoy and even actively seek out the company of other bears of their own sex and age group. One morning in September 1990, Tolya and I climbed to the top of the reflector tower at Cape Blossom. The day was bright, and we could make out thirty-eight bears dotted over an area of less than five acres (2 ha). Fourteen bears occupied a small hollow along the northern beach, where they rested well protected from the wind. Most of them lay between three and fifteen feet (1–5 m) apart, but a few were so close they were touching. Other bears, including a couple of females with cubs, were distributed more widely, lying on day beds in more exposed areas at distances of about fifty to one hundred feet

Polar bears enjoy and even actively seek out the company of other bears of their own sex and age group.

(15–30 m) from each other. A few bears were active and from time to time, one of these approached the sleeping bears, but nothing really significant happened for the first hour. Perhaps the sunny day was making the bears feel too warm to do much.

I was looking at the sleeping bears through my binoculars, when I heard light steps right beneath the platform. I looked down to see a subadult bear suspiciously sniffing the air. Trying to identify its sex, I moved a little and the bear noticed me. Then as Tolya turned to get a better look, he hit a metal part of the platform, frightening the bear away. The escaping subadult (I now knew it was a male) ran quickly past the group of bears in the hollow. They all stood up and looked suspiciously around. A couple of them even started to make for the water but, perhaps seeing no real danger, thought better of it. As I watched the bears settle back down again, I realized that the bears in the hollow were all mature males. Since that incident, I started to pay attention to the way male polar bears socialize in groups.

～

Every season I was on Wrangel Island, mature males formed small resting groups as they waited for the ice to return. I saw such congregations both at Cape Blossom and on Doubtful Spit. Just as the walruses preferred to haul out at the end of the peninsula, so too the polar bears preferred to sleep surrounded by the sea. Also like the walruses, these males chose to rest close to each other. They were obviously attracted not only by the location but also by the presence of other male polar

bears. This could be seen clearly when the groups were forming. As soon as a few bears settled, others would come up and sniff them— sometimes they would even touch noses—and usually they would bed down nearby. I never saw any large male object to others joining him. The attraction between mature males was not limited to these resting groups. I also observed mature males traveling in pairs along the coast, and they often ate together.

This attraction was strong among younger bears, too. In large congregations—for instance, around the mass of dead walruses on Doubtful Spit in 1991—subadults often group together for investigative excursions and play. This happens more often when the bears are well fed and the social situation they find themselves in is calm. The company of other young bears is so attractive that cubs still under their mothers' care often leave the family for several hours to enjoy some freedom with friends.

In 1991, when I was on Doubtful Spit among the dead walruses with Tolya, some assistants from the nearby community arrived in a four-wheel-drive truck to help open the carcasses. The first time we left our truck to work on the carcasses, a band of teenage bears gave the ATV a thorough going-over. They sniffed the doors and windows and then started to push on the glass with their forepaws. We rushed to the truck, and when we were about 150 feet (50 m) from the bears, they abandoned their investigations and seemed to register annoyance at having been interrupted. Another day, I saw the same three bears playing with the carcass of an adult walrus in shallow water near the beach. They swam alongside it, rolled it around in the water, and pushed it at each other.

These three bears were participants in an extraordinary display I witnessed toward the end of my work on Doubtful Spit. We had just finished for the day and were ready to leave. I was sitting in the cab of the truck with the driver, and Tolya was in the truck box with the assistants. We had decided to wait to see whether or not bears would approach the walrus carcasses in our presence. The first bears to approach were the three subadults, who stopped twenty-five feet (8 m) from the truck to investigate the remains of a walrus at the water's edge. Then came a mother bear with one small cub. She was eager to get to the carcasses but was afraid of the truck. Twice she tried to pass, but each time she backed away again. Then she nervously moved forward, passed the subadults, and with her head down, rushed toward the open cab door. Immediately, all three subadults joined her—one on one side, two on the other side of her. All four bears rushed toward us shoulder to shoulder with the cub following behind. About ten feet (3 m) away, they stopped. The female, who was by now excited, hissed and snorted. Then the bears retreated, still keeping in close formation. The team split when the bears reached the edge of the water. The subadults returned to what they had been doing before the female arrived, and the mother and cub went back to the widening of the spit. We left immediately after this incident to let the bears enjoy their evening meal in peace.

This incident showed me an important feature of polar bear social behavior: their ability to cooperate in stressful situations. Closing ranks in the face of danger is a basic feature of socializing in the animal kingdom. The more I observed, the more I came to realize that this kind of social cooperation is normal for this supposedly solitary bear. They joined in groups to escape from me at Cape Blossom when I walked along the spit or when they were being chased down by people in vehicles. The cooperative attack we observed, however, was more than just solidarity in the face of danger, it was active cooperation against a common enemy: the subadults had voluntarily joined a female who was not their mother, and she had left her cub behind.

~

So, is the polar bear a solitary ice wanderer or a more social animal? The scientific definition of a solitary species is one in which individuals keep to their own territories and do not tolerate others of their kind; do not create long-term social bonds; do not develop sophisticated means of socializing with others of their kind and have little interest in doing so; and do not cooperate for routine daily activities. Having watched the bears on Wrangel Island, I have come to the conclusion that they are by nature more social than solitary. We now know that even on the ice, where polar bears spend most of their lives, they are not as solitary as they were once thought to be. If you see a bear on the ice and carefully scan the area, you will often find other bears in the vicinity. Maybe the original misunderstanding arose because polar bears

Having watched the polar bears on Wrangel Island, I conclude that they are more social than solitary by nature.

Winter sun, Wrangel Island
By the end of January, the sun appears above the horizon of Wrangel Island for just a short period every day, shining here through the blowing winter snow along the coastline. With the end of the polar night, the length of the sun's appearance above the horizon rapidly increases with each day.

live on moving Arctic pack ice, an environment where social distance takes on a different meaning from the one most terrestrial predators are familiar with?

From my observations on Wrangel, it seems to me that polar bear society has a hierarchical structure, with mature males at the top. When a mature male appears on the scene, all the other bears pay attention. The general rule is, the more mature, heavier, and stronger the bear, the more dominant it is in any interaction. However, there is another rule that says a bear that approaches confidently and without hesitation is accepted as a potential threat by the bear that is being approached. Even a mature male may be frightened by a young bear under certain circumstances. Polar bears are powerful animals; they are also intelligent. They realize they can hurt one another, and they avoid situations in which their power might be put to the test. They also know that the outcome in any particular situation depends on a bear's personality, current motivation, and individual circumstances. Where possible, they err on the side of caution.

Staying on Cape Blossom or in other areas of traditional polar bear autumn concentrations on the shore, I could see only a part of the polar bear life cycle. How do they manage in other areas and during other seasons? What is going on in their denning habitats in autumn when pregnant females come to land? Or what happens in spring when they emerge from their maternity dens in the snow? To find out I had to live with polar bears in other places, too.

Chapter 7

The Castle of the Snow Queen

The land behind us disappeared in dark gray mist. Our helicopter was flying northeast above the Arctic Ocean, deep into the ice, from Wrangel Island toward Herald Island—the last land between Chukotka and the North Pole. It was October 1, 1992, advanced autumn, when the ocean freezes in this part of the Arctic. A time of fogs, fast weather changes, stormy winds, and much moving of the sea ice.

After twenty minutes, Herald still could not be seen. The helicopter entered dense fog, and pilot Sergei Grunin turned his face to me and crossed his hands to show that there was no way for his machine to go any farther. "We won't find Herald in this damn fog," he said.

At that moment I thought my luck had run out and that my dream of reaching Herald that autumn would not be realized. It was now or never, not only because it would be too expensive to try another time, but also because a flight any later in the season would disturb the mother polar bears who were already arriving on Herald to den and would make me late for the essence of the process I was here to study.

Herald Island
Herald Island looks like an ancient serpent uncoiled in the Arctic Ocean. Winds and the ocean currents permanently tear the ice cover in the vicinity of Herald, thus providing an optimal hunting habitat for polar bears where they can catch seals during any season.

Herald Island camp
The helicopter arrives at our observation camp during a calm, sunny day on Herald.

We stood on the top of Herald Island in the wind and drifting snow with only the polar bears for company.

"Could we try just above water surface?" I asked, hoping against hope that visibility might be better lower down. "We'll see," Sergei answered, flying the helicopter down carefully until we could see dark, cold water and ice only 100 feet (30 m) below. After ten more minutes we emerged from the cloud. Soon the silhouette of a tall cliff appeared. It was partly hidden by mist and torn gray clouds and could not be seen clearly yet, but we had spotted it, and the landing for an experienced pilot was now just a matter of time. My confidence was restored, and a few minutes later we jumped out of the helicopter on the top of a rock in the heart of the High Arctic. I was here to study polar bears, and this season my particular interest was to discover what age and sex of bears would be visiting Herald at this time of year.

In a few minutes, we threw all our luggage out of the helicopter, and it left, disappearing into the misty dark sky in the direction of Chukotka. Tolya Kochnev and I stood on the top of Herald Island in the wind and drifting snow, still hardly believing that we were here at last with only polar bears for company. As far as I knew, we were the first to stay on Herald this far into the autumn. I planned to observe the bears for a couple of weeks, but there was no telling when the helicopter would be able to return, so we had come prepared to stay longer if necessary.

The old cabin 100 feet (30 m) from the edge of the cliff and 500 feet (150 m) above sea level had been built as a field station for the Wrangel Island nature reserve in the 1980s. It was still more or less

Rocky cliffs of Herald Island

Advanced autumn on Herald is a time of permanently stormy weather, and a calm day such as this one is rare. The intense wind permanently tears, pushes, and piles up fields of ice around the island. Polynyas and leads remain around Herald all winter long, thus providing an optimal hunting ground for polar bears where they can catch seals in the open water even in mid-winter. The outfalls of a few small creeks amid the rocky cliffs on the southern coast of Herald are the only route for polar bears to move from the ice up onto the island.

habitable, and we had brought enough materials to repair and renovate it for our stay. The only major damage was a hole in the bottom half of the external door. Since the cabin had been empty for years on a rock occupied by polar bears and exposed to the extremes of the Arctic climate, I had expected much worse. We thanked the bears for their courtesy and commenced our examination of the facilities.

The window covered by a massive wooden shutter had not lost its glass. We took the shutter off and let the twilight enter the room. The oil stove was in good condition, and we had no problem lighting it. The cabin was soon ready to receive its new inhabitants, and we took off our warm clothes, unpacked our rucksacks, and started to celebrate the opening of the autumn season on Herald Island. As night covered the rock, we lit two oil lamps and a candle, filled our glasses with vodka reserved for the occasion, and relaxed to the music of the wind blowing outside. Before that, of course, we had put the shutter back on the window. It would not be nice to wake in the middle of the night to find a curious black nose on the wrong side of the glass.

～

Then next morning we woke up to a dazzling sky. The sun was shining, the air was calm, the temperature was only about 14°F (-10°C), and we could see for miles. Herald was showing itself in its best possible light. We could not know then that that would be one of only two bright days during our three-week stay on the island.

That first day, we made an excursion to the top of the cliff on the northern side of the island and then climbed the mountain that formed the head of the serpent that is Herald. Fresh polar bear tracks were everywhere in the snow. Most areas of deep snow had already been investigated by female bears digging test holes in their search for proper places to make a den. Some of these holes were deep enough to completely hide an adult bear, so we carefully avoided spots we felt might be inhabited. We were anxious not to disturb the animals, who could already have started hibernation.

Despite our good intentions, we did disturb one pregnant female who was lying in a day bed at the foot of a terrace. So hidden was she in her place behind a rock that we did not see her until the last moment, when we were only about sixty feet (20 m) from her. The fat bear rose to her feet looking unhappy and ran heavily along the terrace to escape from these two ugly humans with binoculars. As soon as we saw her, we sat down in the snow to show her that we were not going to give chase. When she disappeared behind the slope, we headed back in the opposite direction. We had decided to call a halt to our excursion so we would not disturb her or other bears any further. We returned to the cabin, got some hot tea, and summarized our first impressions.

Leaving Cape Blossom in autumn
A mature male bear takes his last walk along the coast of Wrangel Island. By the end of October, no bears will remain on the shore. Pregnant females start hibernating; the other bears move onto the ice to hunt seals. This mature male will be active all winter hunting seals along polynyas and leads in the vicinity of Wrangel and Herald Islands.

My first and strongest feeling about Herald was its unbelievable beauty. I fell in love the moment I saw the island, and my affections have never been betrayed.

My first and strongest feeling about Herald was its unbelievable beauty, striking even for a seasoned Arctic traveler like me. I fell in love the moment I saw the island, and my affections have never been betrayed. The second, equally exciting impression was its severity. The tall, jagged, almost vertical cliffs plunged straight down into the cold, dark green water with no beach to break the fall. The countless stony towers and steeples, silvered at the bottom by ice from ocean spray, looked impregnable to the assault of strangers. In January 1914, the *Karluk*, a ship from Vilhjamur Stefansson's expedition, sank to the east of Herald. I could imagine how Captain Bartlett's crew must have felt when they reached this inhospitable rock after a long struggle over ice ridges and open-water leads. Exhausted and frozen, they were greeted by an island on which they could not possibly hope to land.

We were lucky, I thought, to have a cabin on top of the cliff and no need to go down to the ice. The other exciting discovery was that we found no other bears here but fat females coming to hibernate on the rock. Of course, I had expected to see females but, after my experience on Wrangel, I had expected to see mature males and young bears as well. We saw none.

The ice conditions in this region are severe, and many tragedies have occurred here in the history of Arctic exploration. But those same features that make this region so hostile to even well-equipped humans—namely the ice landscape around Wrangel and Herald Islands—are favorable for polar bears. The concentration of bears around Wrangel and Herald Islands is exceptional, but they are not evenly

distributed within the region. Wrangel Island has been thought of as a nursery for polar bears, but after a season on Herald, I could not accept this image any more. The truth is that not Wrangel but Herald must be considered the nursery. Wrangel is more properly the kingdom of the great ice bear, while Herald is a more secret place, the castle of the snow queen.

Even our one-day excursion over a small part of Herald was enough to convince us that we must be extremely careful walking around. There were pregnant females everywhere, and they were supersensitive to any disturbance. The behavior I had employed with polar bears on Cape Blossom could not be applied in the maternity denning area on Herald Island. After two years of studying bears on Wrangel, I expected bears to be inquisitive, to investigate the cabin several times a day, and to eat any food left outside. Our autumn experience on Herald did not conform to our expectations.

We had brought with us the frozen carcass of a reindeer, cut into pieces and packed into a wooden box. When we arrived, we took the box inside the cabin and put it in the coldest corner of the room to keep it safe from bears. We were sure that if we left the meat outside, bears would eat it the first night. After a few days, we realized that the bears were not even trying to approach the cabin. Indeed, all their tracks showed that they were careful to avoid our dwelling. As soon as they recognized signs of our presence, they turned away. The closest they came was about 200 feet (60 m). That was nothing like the pattern

On the top of Herald Island
The top of Herald is exposed to all extremes of unpredictable Arctic weather. Deep snow on mountain slopes is a key factor for successful overwinter denning of pregnant females. The highest mountain top of Herald is several hundred meters above sea level. This area remote from the coast plays host for some denning females too, and the density of maternal dens on Herald is the highest known anywhere in the world.

The ice conditions at Herald are severe, and many tragedies have occurred here in the history of Arctic exploration. But those same features that make this region so hostile to humans are favorable for polar bears.

for the bears at Cape Blossom, with the possible exception of some mature males, who can also be sensitive. Finally, when the meat started to thaw, we put the box outside. Much to our surprise, not a single bear even came to smell the meat. It was clear that pregnant females were fat and cautious, and in no need of any further sustenance.

The weather on the second and subsequent days on Herald had nothing in common with the shining performance we had witnessed on our first day. Wind, snow, and fog became our constant companions. Our view was mostly white or, when the nearest rocks could be seen through the blizzard, grayish-white with some black spots. We took advantage of short gaps of clearer visibility to make more excursions and continue our observations. As most of the females occupied the upper slopes, the only way we could leave the cabin to visit remote parts of the island without disturbing them was by walking along the southern edge of the cliff. Fresh bear tracks and plenty of Arctic fox prints showed that we were not the only ones using this route. Luckily, as autumn advanced, the bears on Herald became less active—and yet, we could not completely avoid unintentional meetings.

On October 15, after five days of a severe gale, we took advantage of a short gap of calm weather to investigate the narrow southern valley. There were only three or four places where bears could climb up onto the island, and this was one of them. The path the bears used was a waterfall in spring. In winter the eroded rock filled with deep snow that was easy to climb up and slide down—at least for bears. In autumn when snow cover was still sparse, it was incredible to see polar bears lifting themselves up over these icy cascades as easily as I might climb a ladder. Today we wanted to check to see if any new bears had arrived after the storm.

We walked slowly down the valley carefully avoiding any patches of deep snow. As the slope descended, the valley narrowed. Nearer to the base we could no longer zigzag but had to go straight down with deep snow on both sides of the canyon wall a mere thirty to fifty feet (10–15 m) on either side of us. I went first; Tolya followed some eighty feet (25 m) behind.

Suddenly, out of the corner of my eye, I noticed a movement. There was something big and yellow sixty feet (20 m) away in a snowy hollow on my right. A polar bear, of course! I had not noticed the hollow until I drew level with it. The bear had her head down while she dug a hole. Immediately I dropped to the ground and tried to retreat before she got frightened. I crawled like a snake on my belly and signaled to Tolya to stop and turn back. But it was too late. The noise of dry snow under our boots had given us away.

The bear lifted her head, looked at us with surprise and fear, and hissed so loudly that I thought she was going to turn herself inside out. I felt guilty. Obviously distressed, she gazed at us for some seconds before climbing the steep slope on the opposite side of the valley, still hissing. She was fat and heavy and could not move fast. She had to go some distance to get out of sight, and I decided to show her that we

Polar bear on the ice
Typically, pregnant females den in October, but some arrive at the denning territory on Wrangel and Herald as early as the beginning of September, where they settle in their snow dens and wait for the winter snow to fall. Female bears may first reproduce when they are four to five years old. A female typically gives birth once every three years, and during her life, may have six to seven litters totaling ten to fifteen cubs.

The bear lifted her head, looked at us with surprise and fear, and hissed so loudly that I thought she was going to turn herself inside out.

were going to run away and not chase her. We pretended to be afraid and started to climb the opposite slope, nervously looking back over our shoulders. I cannot say whether our deception worked or whether it was just the increasing distance between us, but soon she stopped for a few seconds, examined us more calmly and carefully, not hissing any longer, and then continued on her way until she disappeared.

I was sorry to have disturbed the mother bear and hoped she might return to this comfortable spot, but that was a false hope. The next spring when I returned to Herald to continue my observations, I checked this valley regularly but found no maternity den in the hollow.

Main valley of Herald Island
The main valley was well protected from northern winds, and as many as ten females settled here for hibernation during that winter. This was the view from my observation point where I spent many days watching the denning bears.

The cabin was shaking so much in the severe snowstorm and intense winds that, awaking in the night, I thought the cabin was being blown along the rock, and in a few seconds, we would roll down the cliff.

The day after this incident, we found fresh bear tracks over the footprints we had left the previous day—a bear had followed us all the way back to the cabin, turning away some 650 feet (200 m) from the dwelling. Was it the same bear? Had she, in turn, tracked those two awful-smelling creatures that had disturbed the calm of her valley?

The female bears socialized much better among themselves than they did with us. One day we tried to enter the "tail of the dragon"—the narrow northwestern ridge of the island where we had often spotted polar bears. It was a foggy day, and we expected to walk most of the distance hidden from polar bear eyes. When we reached the side of the hollow that separated the tail of the dragon from the head, the fog suddenly lifted. We found ourselves facing a slope where four bears were enjoying the fresh snow. Fortunately, we were not too close. One bear was sliding down the soft snow, a second was approaching a third lying on her day bed, and the last was slowly walking up the slope. We stood watching the group as the fog once again hid the scene. The performance was over, and the path to the ridge was now closed. We returned to the cabin.

By the time we arrived on Herald, no wildlife remained except polar bears, a few Arctic foxes, and a raven. We deduced the presence of the foxes from their tracks. We never actually saw any, although we did hear one crying wistfully in the dusk. The raven was the custodian of the cliffs. Every day when the wind was not too strong, he was out patrolling the island slopes, soaring above our cabin, and croaking his warning of loneliness and danger.

As autumn advanced, the snowstorms increased. We had radio contact with the main office of the nature reserve on Wrangel once a day, but during gales from the northwest they could not receive our signals. Sometimes we could not hear them either. On October 11, the third day of a severe snowstorm, the wind speed exceeded 86 mph (144 km/h). At the top of Herald it reached a speed of 108 mph (180 km/h). That night was not at all comfortable. The heavy cabin was shaking so much on its metal base that, awaking in the night, I thought the

cabin was being blown along the rock, and in a few seconds, we would roll down the cliff. The stove did not warm up the room even with the double door closed. Then we encountered an even more severe problem. Our toilet facilities were outside and once, when one of us tried to get out, the wind tore away the external door. We both jumped to catch it and managed to replace it only after an intense fifteen-minute fight with the flying door. Had we failed, it would have been impossible to keep the cabin warm.

For our last five days on Herald, we were snowbound and had no radio contact with Wrangel at all. Not surprisingly, people there were getting increasingly nervous about our chances of survival on the rock. The weather on Wrangel was now fine, and they had no way of knowing that we were sitting in an unrelenting gale. They imagined the worst, and on October 22, the director of the reserve asked the border service to rescue us in their specially equipped helicopter. Our autumn adventure on Herald Island was over.

That winter we read a newspaper article about how the brave border service had rescued a couple of terrified biologists who were sitting in a cabin besieged by aggressive polar bears. One more negative myth about polar bears had been put into circulation.

But for me that was not the end of adventure. The snow queen with her yellowish-white fur coat and black nose had captured my heart. I had to return.

Wind over Herald Island

The main backbone ridge of Herald forms a barrier against the wind and the harsh Arctic weather it carries. Shielded by this ridge, the main valley on Herald is at least partly safe from the most severe northwest winds and thus provides perfect denning conditions for females. There was a seemingly constant chilly wind and blowing snow streaming over the slopes; this we considered "good" weather for Herald. "Bad" weather conditions would be a blowing gale.

The snow queen with her yellowish-white fur coat and black nose had captured my heart. I had to return to Herald.

Chapter 8

A Time of Cubs

Spring in the Arctic is a festival of light. In March the sun is already high in the sky. Night is getting shorter, and from early morning to late evening, light reflected from the virgin snow fills the air. Spring on Wrangel and Herald Islands is also the time of polar bear cubs. Suddenly one sunny day it is as if a wizard has touched the slumbering land with a wand. Holes start opening in the snow on the pristine slopes, and as if by magic, yellow bears appear with their playful cubs.

In the spring of 1993, I continued my Herald experience. On March 17, a helicopter dropped me and my wife, Irina, on the top of Herald rock. We had arrived just in time: the first females were about to emerge from their maternity dens. For the next five weeks, we observed the private life of polar bears in the most secret area of their native land. The observations of the previous autumn had laid the groundwork for this spring season. I was here to find out what kinds of territorial organization female polar bears develop within their denning areas.

In comparison with Wrangel Island, which has a high density of denning females, Herald is just plain overcrowded. We did not know it when we landed, but this spring there were fourteen dens within half a mile (1 km) of the cabin.

Emerging from the den, Herald Island
The first females emerge from their maternity dens on Wrangel and Herald Islands in early March, but the majority emerge in the last days of March and the beginning of April. Holes open in the pristine snow, and as if by magic, yellow bears appear with their playful newborn cubs.

Observation blind, Herald Island

My wife, Irina Menushina, watches the denning females from our snow blind erected above the southern bay of Herald. This main observation snow blind was situated above this steep slope, offering a perfect view of the denning valley and the ice. At all times when observing the denning females and their cubs—even when watching them from our cabin—my wife and I wore white camouflage clothing to avoid the risk of disturbing the bears at the critical period when they are emerging from their dens. Disturbance of any kind may force a mother to leave her den for the ice too early, at a stage when cubs are not strong enough to follow their mother, probably causing the death of the cub.

From the beginning of the research, I took all possible precautions to avoid upsetting the bears' normal activities. Irina and I both clearly understood our responsibility to keep out of the mother bears' way when they are so vulnerable. Before the mass of females emerged, I piled blocks of snow into a tall wall around the entry to the cabin. All our living facilities were situated inside this wall so that bears would not see us, should we need to come out when they were around. When the females started to appear, we also wore white clothes when we were outside to camouflage ourselves in order to disturb them as little as possible.

As soon as the wall was completed, I hurried to prepare igloo-like blinds. I selected locations with as broad a view as possible of areas where I expected dens to open soon. Altogether I put up eight blinds looking out onto the northern and southern valleys and the upper terraces—those areas with the deepest snow where the digging activity of bears the previous autumn had been highest. Most of these blinds were no more than several hundred feet (a few hundred meters) from the cabin. The nearest one, which as it turned out was to be my main workplace for the next five weeks, was only 300 feet (100 m) from the door. I could reach it quickly by walking along the edge of the cliff and then down the steep slope. The risk of being seen by watchful mother bears on the way from the cabin to the blind was minimal. Of course, it took some time to build the blinds in the first place; however, I solved that problem by building the blinds under the cover of snowstorms, which occurred frequently during the first few weeks of our stay.

Observation camp, Herald Island
Preparing myself and my camp for working and living on Herald in the spring, I built a wall from snow blocks around the door and much of the cabin so that females would not be disturbed by the sight of people coming and going around the cabin. All of our essential living facilities were inside this snow wall—which also protected us from the wind. (Photo by Irina Menushina)

I completed all the necessary preparations in a short time. Now I had to spend hours every day sitting in the blinds waiting for the bears. In spring, mother bears take their time: as long as the weather is still very cold, they are content to sleep in their dens, waiting for conditions outside to improve. For the five weeks we were on Herald, the wind blew unceasingly at about 30 to 60 mph (50–100 km/h) and the temperature ranged from -22 to -4°F (-30 to -20°C). It took until mid-April for the temperature to warm to a balmy 5°F (-15°C). Sometimes I could hardly reach the blind, which was situated on a steep slope covered with a hard icy crust. I often had to get down on all fours so the wind did not blow me down the slope. As I sat in the blind for hours observing the wind getting stronger and stronger, I had plenty of time to nurture doubts about my chances of getting back to the cabin when my observations were over. When the females started coming out, however, I forgot all my discomforts, so interesting and unusual were the events I witnessed.

For the five weeks we were on Herald, the wind blew unceasingly at about thirty to sixty miles per hour (50–100 km/h) and the temperature ranged from -22 to -4°F (-30 to -20°C).

The day after our arrival on Herald, we woke up to blowing whiteness. On the third day, the wind died down, and the first bears started to appear. At two o'clock in the afternoon on March 20, the first calm evening after the blowing gale, on the terrace nearest to the cabin, I noticed small pieces of snow being pushed up to the surface from beneath. It was a sure sign that there was a den under the crust—the female had made a breathing hole. The den was in direct view of the

A black nose appeared from the den hole to sniff the air. Then a head appeared and a mother bear pushed herself through. Following her came another head, a tiny copy of the first— the curious face of her cub.

Emerging from the den, Herald Island
The first emergence of the mother bear from the maternity snow den in spring is a long process. After a winter of hibernating and giving birth to her cubs in December or January and then spending two more months in the den with her cubs, the mother must dig out through all of the winter's accumulation of snow. Before emerging into the outside world, a black nose first appears through the cleared den hole to check out the surroundings by sniffing the air for any danger and to check weather conditions. The female may spend many minutes smelling for foreign scents before she then pokes her full head outside and then pushes herself through the narrow entrance. Females often then stop halfway through the den hole to visually scan the scene. When she is finally outside of the den, a second bear head—a tiny copy of the first one—appears behind her. The new cub emerges to look at the outside world for the first time. The first emergence from the den usually occurs in calm weather, often after a snowstorm, when a pristine quiet enwraps the Arctic mountains.

cabin, and I could keep an eye on it any time except at night.

The next morning before sunrise, I loaded myself into the blind nearest to this den. I had just settled in when a black nose appeared from the hole, which had been widened since I first saw it the previous day. The nose sniffed the air for a few minutes and then disappeared. In no time at all, a head appeared and a mother bear pushed herself through the narrow entry. She sat down and scanned the air with her sensitive nose. Following her came another head, a tiny copy of the first—the curious face of her cub.

I recognized the mother right away as an old bear. She was tall and gaunt and looked as though she needed to go out onto the ice to hunt soon; however, it would be difficult for her cub to make such an adventurous journey until it was bigger. The mother spent half an hour sniffing the air and checking out the surroundings before diving back into the den head first. Her cub, which was sitting on its rump, disappeared into the den as its mother descended back into the snow. During the next three hours, they appeared briefly one more time, but again the mother did not move from the entrance of the den. That was all I saw of the bear we later came to know as Professor on this, the first day of our acquaintance. She lay low for the following two days while I discovered several other opened dens.

Another snowstorm kept the eager females at bay for two more days. When it stopped, on March 27, they emerged en masse. Besides Professor, two other bears appeared with their cubs on the terraces right above the cabin. They dug snow and ate grass to clean and start their intestines. They also watched each other but kept their distance.

The first thing I saw when I glanced out of the cabin the next morning was Professor passing only 160 feet (50 m) in front of our wall of snow. She glanced at the cabin and continued walking in a purposeful fashion as if she had decided to leave for the ice. Her cub followed her like a little rolling ball, sliding down the slippery slope and jumping up on its legs again. She did not even look back at it, although later I was to discover what a careful mother she was.

After Professor left her den, it remained unoccupied, so I decided to focus my observations on the northern valley where many other dens were opening. It turned out to be a good decision. The valley was narrow and well protected from the prevailing winds. Mothers could be active here even on windy days, and I had a clear view of this popular denning site from my blind.

March 28 brought new acquaintances. I saw four different mothers with cubs, and a new den was opened on the northern slope of the valley only 230 feet (70 m) from my blind. A mature female with two cubs—one a clean, pure white and the other a dirty gray—came to graze on the grass along the valley bottom. I had seen this mother the

Intruders, Herald Island

The maternity den of the female I called Snowflake was situated directly above the creek bottom used by other females as the main route to go grazing and to reach the outfall. There was too much disturbance for Snowflake. Every time she wanted to let her cubs out, another female appeared in the valley. Snowflake rushed back to her den's entry and "locked" the entrance by blocking it with her body to keep her cubs safe inside.

day before on the terraces and had given her the name Pozemka (which means "streaming snow"). Pozemka went up the valley and disappeared from my view, and Professor appeared on the scene. She came from the edge of the creek, where the valley falls abruptly to the sea. Perhaps she had visited the ice and climbed back up to the rock, or maybe she had just been resting on a day bed at the edge of the cliff beyond my view. This hollow is one of only four passes along which mothers with small cubs can leave the rock. Later I discovered that this northern pass was one of the two with the highest level of polar bear activity on the island. Not only bears who had denned in the valley, but also some from remoter areas used this route. I was in the perfect position to observe all bear movements around this outlet.

I soon got to know other families. By April 1, there were six open dens in the northern valley in direct view of my blind. Three more were on the right slope of the hollow that was out of view. The female from the den nearest to my blind was young, pretty, and shy. I named her Snowflake. For a long time I saw no sign of her cubs. Nearly every day she popped her head out of the den to look around. Maybe she was waiting for a quiet moment to lead out her cubs; however, there was no peace and quiet in this corner of the High Arctic—there was constant movement of polar bears along the bottom of the canyon.

The upper cirque of the valley—a steep-walled semicircular bowl—was occupied by a mature pure white female with two cubs. She came out for the first time on March 24, and then spent most of her time resting on some big stones near the top of the northeastern point. I could see her clearly from the door of the cabin. The area was well protected from the wind, so she was often outside even when a blizzard forced other families to escape into their dens. I gave her the name Snow Queen.

A few days later, two other young females appeared—Northern Rose and Yellow Coat. Northern Rose had a den on the right slope that was out of my sight. I saw her for the first time on March 30 when she came out to graze at the creek bed. She was still quite fat and had a couple of strikingly cute ball-like cubs that, during their first days outside, were slightly pink. She lived in the area for nineteen days after she first emerged from her den.

Yellow Coat was the last of the bears I observed to appear. Her den was situated in the upper cirque beneath two other dens that had opened earlier. I saw her only twice before she left. She had two cubs, but she did not let them out of the den until the whole family headed for the ice. I think the reason she kept the cubs under wraps and then made a dash for the ice was that she was frightened of Snow Queen, her closest neighbor.

～

Once the bears started to move around, I had to be in the blind early in order not to miss important events. Mother bears get up with the sun, and every morning the first families were in the valley by seven. Each family filled its day in roughly the same way. First, the mother walked with her cubs down the valley to the cliff. Usually, she would head directly to the edge, where she would stop and sniff the ocean. All the bears paid incredible attention to the sea. Every day they could leave their dens, they spent many minutes at the end of the valley sniffing, listening, and watching the ocean.

They also checked the ice conditions from the upper cliffs by listening to the ice and smelling the open leads. I noticed that when the wind carried the fresh smell of the sea—even I could smell it with my weak nose—the females got excited and went to the edge, pointing their noses out to sea. They did not leave the rock right away, however. They were patiently waiting for their cubs to get stronger.

After checking the condition of the sea, each female turned back and walked slowly up the valley, grazing on grass. I was surprised to see how long they grazed every day and how much grass they consumed. Pozemka, for instance, came out of her den on March 20 and lived in the denning area until April 4. For these two weeks, she only entered the den at night or to escape from a blizzard. Every day she was out, I saw her grazing. On March 31, for instance, she appeared in the valley at 8:30 A.M. grazed for ninety-five minutes, took a break for fifteen minutes to nurse her cubs, then continued grazing for forty more minutes. I observed Professor grazing for eleven of the twenty-one days she lived in the area. Other females followed similar patterns, consuming an incredible quantity of grass. The bears reminded me of hungry cows. Later, when we examined their feces, they consisted entirely of

There was no peace and quiet in this corner of the High Arctic—there was constant movement of polar bears along the bottom of the canyon.

grass. The cubs were eating grass, too.

Despite these similar routines, individual differences between females in habits, behavior, and attitudes toward each other were remarkable. Like other bears, Snowflake looked out from her den early in the morning. Usually, she just put her head out and watched the surroundings. If there were no other bears in sight, she might come out and sit at the entry or roll in the snow around the den to clean her fur; however, she could never enjoy being out for long. In no time at all, another mother would appear, leading her cubs along the bottom of the valley. Immediately, Snowflake would rush back to her den, close the entry with her body, and then watch the visitor for a while before diving back into the den.

I was curious to know how many cubs Snowflake had. Every time I thought she was ready to call her cubs out, another female would appear and Snowflake would sit on the entrance to the den and not let the cubs out. Sometimes she even had to force them back into the den by pushing them with her nose. The first time I saw her cubs was on April 2. Snowflake came out and three small heads appeared anxiously in the entry, looking around with curiosity and fear.

Snowflake lived in her den for fifteen days after opening it. She came out several times a day; however, only once did I see her leave her cubs alone in the den while she went down to the creek to eat some grass. I never saw her take her cubs along with her to graze before they finally left for the ice. In those fifteen days, I saw the cubs only five times. As I was to discover, Snowflake had good reason to be wary of other females.

∼

Nearly every day, I observed at least one territorial interaction between females—a kind of competition for dens. I found out that a female may use several dens if she comes across empty ones after having emerged from her own. Some dens were constantly in demand and used by several females in turn. Only mature females, however, changed dens. For instance, I saw Professor occupy three dens besides her own. The average number of dens used by mature bears was at least two to three, but I never saw a young female using any den besides her own. Young females ranked low in the settlement and were somewhat afraid of the older ones. This being the case, if the owner of a den carelessly left it to make a long excursion, she might return to find the den occupied by an intruder. The bears knew this and took precautions. Once, on April 3, I watched Snow Queen guard her den against Pozemka.

As usual, Snow Queen was resting on her day bed of stones. Her cubs were enthusiastically playing around. Polar bear cubs put on a magnificent performance when they play, and their play is so entirely joyful that I can watch it for hours. I was captivated by this wonderful show, when I noticed Pozemka climbing up to the cirque from the creek. She reached the smooth plateau of the cirque and walked slowly toward the upper slope and Snow Queen's den. Snow Queen watched.

Moving from one patch of grass to another, Pozemka was slowly

First steps, Herald Island
Two small polar bear cubs take their first steps into the outside world alongside their mother. The area around the maternity den is a living environment for the family. A few days after first opening the den to the world, each mother bear makes a deep day bed in the snow near the den and spends some time there exposing the cubs to the warm sunshine and letting them play. If there are no predators or other bears about to disturb them, females may live at their dens for two to three weeks, waiting until the cubs are strong enough to follow their mother out onto the ice.

Polar bear cubs put on a magnificent performance when they play, and their play is so entirely joyful that I can watch it for hours. I was captivated by this wonderful show.

approaching the den. Now Snow Queen was getting nervous. She sat up on her day bed, staring intently at the intruder, then she rushed to her den. Immediately, her cubs interrupted their play and quickly followed their mother. Pozemka headed toward the slope and passed to the left of the den. As soon as Snow Queen realized that Pozemka was not going to try to take over her den, she quieted down, slowly approached the entrance, and sat in it. This time the incident was over; however, Snow Queen's den was attractive to other females, and she had to be constantly on her guard against competitors.

Professor was the bear most interested in other females' dens. She was among the first to emerge and the last to leave. She watched the other bears in the settlement as if doing her own research parallel to mine, and she was always on the lookout for a chance to enter their dens. I was most excited to witness a dramatic episode between Professor and Snowflake. It was a case of an older mother putting social pressure on a younger one.

Observation cabin, Herald Island
During a heavy snowstorm, my wife and I are confined to our cabin, where we catch up on paperwork, making notes on our observations.

As I waited every day for Snowflake to come out with her cubs, I saw Professor grazing at the creek and investigating the condition of the ice. For a while, Professor did not approach Snowflake's den; however, she soon changed her tactic. The first time Professor appeared on the snow beneath Snowflake's den was on March 30. The older female made her day bed 130 feet (40 m) below the den. Snowflake did not see her when she came out to roll in the snow. Then she sensed the intruder, went down the slope to investigate, and when she saw Professor resting so close, she hissed, rushed back to the den, and blocked the entrance with her body.

Again, on April 6, Professor rested on the snow beneath Snowflake's den. Again the young female was frightened and escaped inside the den. The next day, Snowflake let her cubs out and led them sixty feet (20 m) from the entry to rest on the open day bed. No sooner had she relaxed then Professor appeared at the creek below, walking to the edge of the cliff. Immediately, Snowflake rushed back to the den, leading her cubs inside and even pulling the smallest one in by the scruff of his neck.

Snowflake's cubs were still too small to leave for the ice, but the next day she tried to lead them down from the den anyway. The cubs refused to follow and she had to return. I was anxious not to miss the moment when she led her cubs away. Then a severe snowstorm started. This would give me a break, I thought, until the gale was over.

The wind died down early on the morning of April 12. I was in the blind with the last gusts at 6:50 A.M. I was sure that Snowflake would not lead her small cubs out in that terrible gale. All dens were closed with snow except Snowflake's, but fresh snow in the entry proved the owner had not been out yet. At 7:17, a female looked out from the hole, but there was something strange about her. She spent eight minutes at the entry and then went back in, leaving me confused.

I spent five more hours waiting. At 12:47 P.M., she reappeared. This time she came out, spent some time at the entry, and then led her one cub away. Where were the other two? I was so certain that only Snowflake could be inside this den, that it had never occurred to me that another female might take her place. And yet this is what had happened. The new owner of the den was Professor.

I spent three and a half more hours waiting without success to see Professor come back to the den. Suddenly, at 4:04 P.M., I heard soft steps on the snow behind me. I turned to see her only eighty feet (25 m) away. She was approaching the blind by following my usual trail. Unsure of her intentions, I turned to face her and showed myself a little. As soon as she saw me, an expression of distaste appeared on her face. She stopped, looked at me for a few seconds, then walked away across the slope followed by her cub.

No other female appeared near Snowflake's den for the rest of the day. Snowflake had gone. I never saw her again. What amazed me most was that she had led her cubs away in a blizzard probably because the chance of meeting other females was lowest under such weather conditions.

When I came back to the cabin, Irina told me that a quarter of an hour earlier Professor had come up to the cabin and sniffed our tracks around the snow wall. Then she had followed my trail for a few yards and laid down on the snow 160 feet (50 m) from the cabin with her head toward the entry. She waited for some time until Irina came out and Professor could see her. Then the bear started along the trail sniffing my tracks. She got to the point where the slope falls away abruptly. If she had continued along the trail, she would not have been able to see me had I walked up the slope. Here she turned aside, made a loop, and approached the trail from the side so that she could see anything moving along the trail. From this point she still could not see the rest of the trail and the blind. She repeated the same maneuver as before and rejoined the trail lower down just in view of the blind. This way, she was careful to avoid an unexpected confrontation with me. We discovered all this by tracking her movements afterward. I did not doubt that she counted us and then carefully planned her next move. She watched the cabin, and when she realized that there was one human being in it and fresh tracks leading away from the dwelling, she checked them out to see whether or not the other human being was sitting in the blind.

Professor's investigative interests were not limited to Snowflake or to us. No one in the settlement escaped her attention. One time I saw her pushing Northern Rose from a day bed. Another time I observed her competing for Snow Queen's den with a mature female who used it after Snow Queen had left. Professor was always around when there was something going on. The last time I saw her was on April 17. She was one of the last bears to leave the rock that spring. By the end of April, Herald had been abandoned by the bears, whose life stories continued on the ice.

Suddenly, I heard soft steps on the snow behind me. I turned to see the bear only eighty feet (25 m) away. She was approaching the blind, following my usual trail.

Chapter 9

On the Ice

We were woken at 6:05 A.M., April 4, 1993, by knocking and scratching at the window of our cabin on Herald Island. Somebody was trying to remove the wooden shutter. In this remote part of the High Arctic, the visitor had to be a polar bear, but the uninvited guest was too active and forthright to be a mother with cubs. Standing on his hind legs, the adult male bear pushed on the shutter with his paws and loudly sniffed the warm air streaming through chinks in the window frame. I was thankful that I was in the habit of covering the window with the shutter every night even though the female bears had never approached the cabin. After a few seconds, the bear circled the cabin, inspected our wall of snow, and returned to the window. This time he applied more force.

The shutter was shaking terribly. To lose the glass would be too high a price to pay for the privilege of spending a few more minutes in a warm sleeping bag. Damning the bear's investigative enthusiasm, I jumped up and pulled on some clothes to go out. The bear heard me and stopped fighting the shutter. When I came out of the cabin, he was 300 feet (100 m) away walking in the direction of the creek. He glanced back at me and headed off down the slope. The time of cubs on Wrangel and Herald Islands is also the time for polar bear courtship on the surrounding ice. Every spring some males come inland to check for female tracks. The appearance of the guest near our cabin on April 4 was all part of polar bear social routine.

On the ice, Herald Island
When hunting or traveling on the ice, polar bears often hide behind ice floe ridges and survey the surroundings.

Female bears in heat mark prominent pieces of snow with urine to help interested males locate them. On Herald, I found a few of these marks even on the high plateau once the season of love had begun. Males may also be able to detect the scent of a receptive female just by testing the air. Polar bears are known to have the most sensitive noses in the animal kingdom, although they way they might communicate through odors has not been adequately studied. All year round, as bears wander over the ice or scout the shorelines, they pay great attention to tracks in the snow. They constantly move their noses from side to side to explore their surroundings. This important habit allows them to recognize the slightest signs of another bear—or a potential source of food—in their cold, virginal ice environment.

~

April 4 was a sunny day with a light breeze. When I went down to begin my observations, I found a couple of bears together on the ice just below the cliffs. I soon discovered that when there is a female in estrus within the area, there are usually several males around. That spring, I observed a total of four courting couples. In each case, there was another male waiting in the wings. Perhaps that explains why the couples I observed never remained in one spot for more than a few hours.

Although I did not observe fights between male polar bears, they are known to compete fiercely for females, sometimes drawing blood. The scars on the faces of male polar bears bear witness to these fights. Surprisingly, I saw few such scars on the mature males on Wrangel. It may be that mating couples can take refuge from aggressive third parties behind the many ice ridges that form around the island. It may also be that there are larger numbers of available females to males here than there are in other regions of the Arctic.

I was surprised to see how gentle the couples were with one another. They walked together everywhere, usually with the male following the female. The female would often look back as if inviting the male to follow, especially if he seemed to be getting too engrossed in sniffing tracks on the snow. While walking and resting, the couple would often rub up against each other, sniff and lick each other's lips and noses, and roll together in the snow.

Once, on April 18, I noticed a couple of bears swimming across a small lakelike polynya toward Herald. The window of open water, about 650 feet (200 m) wide, was starting to freeze, and the bears had to break through the fresh ice. For the first half of the way, the male acted as an icebreaker. Then, perhaps finding this work too exhausting, he started to dive under the ice, coming to the surface every ten feet or so (a few meters), making breathing holes in the ice with his head. The female followed, popping up through the same holes one step behind. On the last half of the way, she seemed to lose patience and started making her

Sunshine over the freezing ocean
All year round, both Herald and Wrangel Islands serve as icebreakers slicing through the drifting polar ice. Here, permanent leads along the eastern coast of Herald may change in size and width in a few minutes.

Polar bears are known to have the most sensitive noses in the animal kingdom. Their sense of smell allows them to recognize the slightest signs of another bear or a potential source of food in their cold, virginal ice environment.

116

own line of breathing holes parallel to his. In this fashion, the couple reached the opposite side of the polynya, hauled out on the pack ice just below my observation point, and continued their courtship.

~

Mother bears leaving Herald were leading their cubs into a community of courting couples and single mature males hunting seals and looking for female bears in heat. During their first weeks out in the world, polar bear cubs are absolutely helpless and vulnerable to all environmental and social extremes. To what extent might adult males be dangerous for these small cubs? Pack ice is a harsh environment, and I was particularly anxious to see the cubs' first steps on this unpredictable, drifting continent.

It is a common misconception that male polar bears are aggressive and hunt and kill cubs of their own species. Although I have viewed hundreds of interactions between polar bears in the autumn, I have never seen a mature male threaten or attack a female with cubs. Even the scientific literature reports that predation by mature males is a factor in cub mortality, although my examination of the literature has not unearthed any objective evidence of this terror. The only examples I found reported situations when somebody had found tracks showing that one bear had been eating another. In the Canadian Arctic, for instance, scientists observed a male eating the fresh carcass of a female while her yearling cubs looked on. The inference was made that the male had killed the mother while she was trying to defend her cubs. It

Mother bear and playing cubs, Herald Island
With their mother watching over them, a trio of cubs plays on the slope around their den. Different females often use the same dens, taking over the den in their turn after another mother is finished with it.

Male polar bears are known to compete fiercely for females, sometimes drawing blood. The scars on the faces of male bears are evidence of these fights.

Above: Maternity day bed, Herald Island
After emerging from their snow dens, the females paid particular attention to the ocean, checking conditions for hunting. The bears often made their day beds at the edge of steep cliffs from which they could watch the ice.

Right: Exploring Herald Island
The daily activity of each polar bear family usually followed the same routine centered on the sea and ice conditions. Here, a mother leads her cub to the outfall of a creek, the gate to the ocean. After a look at the sea, the mother turned back and headed up the valley to graze. On each calm day, when the weather allowed the mother bear to take her cubs out of the den, females grazed along the valley bottom where the adults and their small cubs consumed a large amount of dry grass. I believe the females eat grass to clean their intestines after hibernation and also for food until they can go hunting. Cubs seem to eat grass simply because their mother does, but they also drink their mother's milk, and as soon as their mother gets meat, they begin eating meat, too. Typically, cubs nurse until they are two years old.

seems to me more likely that the male found the dead female and ate the carcass as carrion. The actual cause of the mother's death could have been disease, starvation, or a bullet wound. It is not surprising that the cubs had not left her. Cub-mother social bonds are strong, especially between mothers and young cubs who cannot survive without a mother's care. On Cape Blossom, for instance, I observed a mother who would not leave the body of her dead cub for days.

～

Polar bear females are good mothers. They take great care of their cubs and bravely defend them at the first sign of danger, apparent or real. If a male happens to walk toward the mother, she immediately calls her cubs to her side, and they stand together in a compact group rather like a defensive stand of musk-oxen. If the male gets too close, the mother rushes to attack him with open mouth and often strikes him and pushes him with her forepaw. She might even bite him.

I have also observed females with cubs approach mature males and initiate the attack. The males replied either with soft defensive threat displays or made good their escape. After all I have learned about polar bears, I cannot believe that even a strong male would take on a mature female, who is a powerful predator in her own right. It would just be too dangerous. But if males are not a threat, why then are polar bear mothers so suspicious of them?

I offer an alternative interpretation of the polar bear mother's fear of mature males. If female bears are good mothers, which they are, we should expect precisely this behavior of them. Good mothers should protect their cubs against any potentially risky interaction. They should avoid situations in which their cubs might get hurt. Polar bears are powerful animals, and their social interactions are sometimes aggressive. What is trivial for an adult bear might be serious for a cub. Polar bears realize the power of their own species, and from their childhood, they have learned to respect it.

I believe, therefore, that the mothers' careful behavior does not prove the aggressive nature of the males, but rather the polar bear's ability to avoid potential risks in order to manage its social life in the safest way possible. Females without cubs accept mature males at close quarters much more easily than mothers with cubs, and I often saw both males and females peacefully walking, eating, or resting near each other.

～

Pozemka was the first mother I observed leaving for the ice. At about ten o'clock on the morning of April 4, she followed the creek to the cliff. By eleven she was on the ice walking her cubs along the lead. I saw her approach the open water and bend forward as if showing it to the cubs. Their first reaction was one of fright. They anxiously pressed against each other as they sniffed the strange stuff. Their mother stood nearby watching them. Their fear soon turned to more confident interest. The white cub slipped down into the water and swam at the edge, while the gray hung back with his head down. Pozemka then

Polar bear females are good mothers. They take great care of their cubs and bravely defend them at the first sign of danger, apparent or real.

On the ice, Herald Island

A mother with her two cubs heads toward the ocean, finally leaving the island in late April. The first thing the female does is hunt for a seal. The mother will do her best to kill a seal on her own, but she will also use any chance to get the remains of a seal killed by a male bear. Now is the time to teach cubs to live on the ice, to swim, and to avoid the many dangers that the cubs can meet at any step in this harsh and unforgiving environment.

decided to leave and called the cubs to follow. Gray turned away from the water, but White was helplessly floundering in the lead unable to get out. Pozemka returned, caught him by the skin, and gently pulled him out head first.

No sooner had she returned White to the floe, than Gray started sliding down into the water. Pozemka caught him and pulled him back. Now White wanted in again. Pozemka repeated the catch-and-pull exercise. She tried to lead the cubs away, but as soon as she turned her back, Gray made a beeline for the lead, jumped in, and swam around. Once again Pozemka caught him. At last, she managed to get the cubs away.

The cubs had now gotten a taste of swimming and were eager to try out their new-found skill. Sixty feet (20 m) farther along, the family approached open water again. This time both cubs rushed to the edge without any sign of fear, unhesitatingly jumped in, and swam around. Pozemka looked worried. She caught the wayward cubs and pulled them back one by one. It took some time to get them to follow her. As the family headed away, Pozemka was constantly attentive, keeping a close eye on her surroundings.

Some 300 feet (100 m) farther on, the family came across the fresh tracks of a courting couple. Immediately Pozemka turned aside; however, within a third of a mile (0.5 km) she met these bears. The couple was resting together on the ice after copulation. As soon as the male saw another bear, he got up and rushed toward the intruder. Although his intention seemed to be to defend his female rather than to attack the intruders, his long lunge and loud growl terrified the family.

Pozemka ran away so fast that her cubs could barely keep up with her. Eventually, she did look back and adjust her speed to their pace. The cubs followed their mother as closely as they could. The male stopped after 300 feet (100 m), growled several times, sniffed the family's tracks, and returned to his mate, who was curiously watching the interaction from behind an ice ridge. Although this had been a typical territorial interaction between a male defending the area around his sexual partner and an intruder, Pozemka was wise to beat a hasty retreat as an aggressive, excited male could easily hurt small cubs.

Since that incident, I have watched many mothers on the ice when there were mature males around, but I have never seen a male attempt to chase, hunt, or otherwise aggressively threaten mothers with cubs. In the ever-shifting ice landscape around Herald and Wrangel Islands, mothers with cubs could easily avoid these males, who were far more interested in finding females in heat than in anything else.

~

Even though mother bears might want to keep their distance, there were distinct advantages to being in the same area as hunting males. The emergence of the mother bears and cubs from the maternity dens coincides with the presence of fat, suckling seal pups on the ice. In some areas, polar bears find these seal pups easy prey; however, surveys have shown that in the Wrangel Island region, only a few seal pups are ever found. This may be because severe pressure in the ice causes so many ice ridges. Although masses of seals haul out onto the ice in late May and June, in April seals are hard to find. Mature males have more opportunities to hunt than do females who have small cubs to look after. Males are normally in good shape at this time of the year and from every killed seal consume only the blubber, leaving the carcass for others. Ravens, gulls, and Arctic foxes are not the only ones who survive on these remains—young bears and mothers with cubs do, too.

I watched one of those lucky mothers on April 16. Sitting in the blind as usual, I noticed the resident raven of Herald flying out over the ice. The bird landed one and a quarter miles (2 km) from the cliffs, where I noticed a spot of blood on the snow. Scanning the area with my binoculars, I quickly picked up a second raven at the kill. A few hours earlier, I had watched a male polar bear hunting a seal close to this area. I had just focused on the ravens when both birds flew some yards away as a female polar bear rushed to the remains. It was a mother I had observed two hours earlier as she left for the ice with her three cubs. She chewed hungrily on the carcass a few times, then returned to her cubs, which were huddled together 100 feet (30 m) away. She led the anxious cubs to the kill, and I spent the rest of the afternoon watching the bears and the ravens taking full advantage of the male's largesse.

As soon as the female turned away from the carcass to bring her cubs to the meal, the raven, who had been jumping around her, landed

The raven landed on the carcass and hurried to get his portion. The bear cubs stopped and flattened their bodies against the snow. They were fearful of this strange new thing. As their mother called to them, they cautiously approached.

on the remains and hurried to get his portion. The female quickly returned to the carcass, but her cubs stopped fifteen feet (5 m) away from it and flattened their bodies against the snow. They were fearful of this strange new creature. As their mother called to them, they cautiously approached, with the largest cub in the lead. As the mother stood on one side of the carcass with her cubs huddled up between her legs, the raven was jumping up and down and nervously pecking it from the other. The raven's mate soon joined the group, and the ravens ate from one side of the carcass while the bears fed from the other.

While the raven and bear families were making short work of the leftover seal kill, another mature male was still-hunting for seal only 1,000 feet (300 m) from them in the lead. The fat white male held his head low to a narrow crack in the ice and stood as if frozen to the spot. This was rush hour on the ice indeed, and I could not take my eyes away from my binoculars for a moment.

Meanwhile, after fifteen minutes or so of intensive chewing and pecking, there was not much left of the seal carcass. The mother bear picked up part of the skeleton in her teeth and dragged it off a short distance. Then she dropped the remains behind a large ice floe and left it. The cubs sucked on the bones a little longer and then left with their mother. The raven landed on the remains to finish off the last scraps. One of the cubs, perhaps emboldened by its recent meal, turned as if to attack the raven but stopped anxiously ten feet (3 m) away from the bird. It watched the raven for a few seconds before rejoining the rest of its family.

The carcass devoured, the raven now turned its attention to the hunting male. He had by this time given up on his still-hunt and was walking along the edge of the open lead sniffing the snow. Suddenly, he jumped into the water and disappeared beneath the surface. I could not see what had attracted his attention, and three minutes later he reappeared in the same lead with no sign of prey. As the bear hauled out onto the ice, the raven landed a few yards in front of the bear's nose and watched him attentively. The bear looked at the bird, rose up onto his hind legs, and jumped at the bird to scare it away. The raven took off and landed a few yards farther away from the bear. The bear lunged a couple more times, rolling in the snow after each jump. He then lay down in the snow and simply watched the raven. The bear's hunt had been unsuccessful. But while the male was still in the water, in a neighboring lead only 200 feet (70 m) away, a seal's head had appeared. For about three minutes, the seal had intently watched the spot where the bear had disappeared.

The scenes I had witnessed were only the beginning of the long spring and summer hunting season for polar bears. All bears need to be lucky to have a successful hunt. The survival of those who were not lucky depended on surplus kills made by more skillful hunters. All summer the bears would be on the ice, inaccessible to the curious observer. Only in the autumn would some of them come to the island again, and only then would I be able to renew my observations.

Living on ice
Bears prefer to stay on the ice that forms along the shore. The female with two cubs-of-the-year quietly sleeps on the crashed pack ice, while another family examines the edge of the ice-covered sea.

The bear looked at the raven, rose up onto his hind legs, and jumped at the bird to scare it away. The raven took off and landed a few yards farther away from the bear. The bear lunged a couple more times, rolling in the snow after each jump.

Chapter 10

A Close Encounter

In spite of hard ice around Wrangel and Herald in the spring of 1993, extremely hot weather during the summer resulted in a long season of open water that autumn. This season I was alone and could devote my full attention to the bears. It was my most enjoyable stay on Wrangel; it was also my most productive. The more you get personally acquainted with individual animals, the better you understand them, and the more deeply you assimilate yourself into the community of wild animals, the more directly involved you are in their life drama. This time I could recognize individual bears, and the same group of bears stayed on the beach until mid-October when the ice arrived from the north.

I arrived at Cape Blossom on September 5 to find eleven bears at the end of the spit. With the exception of a couple of subadults, they were big mature males. By the middle of the month, the first females arrived, and by the end of the month, there were about forty animals in the area. After four years of studying polar bears, I found that females with cubs represent up to 32 percent of bears visiting the coast of Wrangel Island, cubs make up to 33 percent of the population, mature males compose 6 to 13 percent, and the balance are immature bears.

Lessons in living, Wrangel Island
Now is the time to teach cubs to live on the ice, to swim, and to avoid the many dangers that the cubs can meet at any step in this harsh and unforgiving environment. Female bears with cubs are the most aggressive members of the polar bear community—but it is a defensive aggression. This mother with her two one-year-old cubs leads an attack to chase away an intruding mature male bear.

I spent forty-seven days out on the peninsula with the bears from dawn until dusk. Every evening I had visitors. Bears looked in the cabin windows when I was writing at the table, got into the cold room when I left the door open, and sniffed and scraped the wooden shutters I closed every night to keep the glass safe from rough wet noses. I found the bears to be courteous visitors who were never rough enough to actually break anything and who always accepted my rights to the camp, leaving the territory as soon I appeared.

Until mid-September, I observed the mostly male "club." As the weeks went by, new animals began arriving. Walking along the coast from the east early in the morning or late each evening, most of them passed my cabin on their way to Cape Blossom, so I could greet each new arrival from my doorstep. In addition to the males, I got to know several subadults, six mothers with cubs-of-the-year, three mothers with yearlings, and five mothers with two-year-old cubs. None of the females with more than one two-year-old cub looked fat enough, whereas the ones with only one cub of this age looked well fed. Only mature females, who presumably had lots of experience in looking after cubs, were followed by third-year cubs. The cost to the female of raising cubs and the cost of maternal care for older cubs was pretty clear. There was even one mother with three third-year cubs. I gave her the name Marfa. She appeared to have a strong, well-balanced character, and her standing and that of her cubs among the other bears in the community was high.

Every day I went out among the bears. Usually, I was dressed in white clothing. I hoped that from a distance the bears would accept me as one of them as I watched and photographed them from my observation post on the spit at the base of the tower. It seemed to work. When the bears approached me to find out whether I was male or female and how old I was, many appeared disappointed to find a human being instead of a bear; however, none of them ever doubted my high social position—except one.

～

The first time I set eyes on her I knew she was going to be a problem. She arrived on September 16, when she led her two third-year cubs past my door. I was sitting outside by the east wall of the cabin. I let her get within fifteen feet (5 m) before I showed myself. She stopped as soon as she saw me and hissed at me loudly. She did not get frightened but slowly turned back to face me, looking very angry indeed. Something about her reminded me of a woman I knew, whose face and figure, when she was angry, looked similar to the bear's. So I named this bear after that woman—Valentina Pavlovna.

On September 24, I took my usual walk from the cabin to the end of the spit, where bears were sitting quietly near the base of the tower. I went to the top of the tower to count them for a while and then came down again to photograph them. As far as the bears were concerned,

Above: Observation camp, Cape Blossom
Winter comes with full fury in the Arctic, bringing snow, ice, and wind to our cabin on Wrangel.

Opposite: Full moon over Wrangel Island
Autumn arrives on Wrangel at the end of August as the nights get long, the days get short, and soon polar night blacks out the sky.

there was nothing unusual about my behavior. Usually, when a bear recognizes my presence, it simply keeps its distance. Some come closer to investigate and then run away as soon as they catch the smell of human. A few come up as near as ten to twelve feet (3–4 m). But before that day I had no serious confrontations with them.

When I was counting bears from the top of the tower, I had noticed that I, too, was being watched—by a mature female resting on a day bed one hundred and fifteen feet (35 m) from the base of the tower. It was Valentina Pavlovna. Her two young cubs were feeding on old walrus skins some sixty to one hundred feet (20–30 m) away.

A close encounter, Cape Blossom
Upon first meeting this mature female, who I called Valentina Pavlovna, I realized that she was an aggressive, strong-willed bear and might be a problem under certain circumstances. Sleeping on a day bed neighboring my small observation cabin sometimes used as a blind at the top of the spit, Valentina Pavlovna was always watchful and ready to protect her cubs. Upon sighting me, she angrily jumped up to attack.

When they came back to join her, Valentina Pavlovna bit the female cub on the neck when she tried to sniff her mother's nose. The cub immediately lay down and the second cub, a male, put himself between his angry mother and his punished sister. Obviously, Valentina Pavlovna was in a bad mood. When Valentina Pavlovna had calmed down a little, all three bears lay down together on the same day bed. When I came down from the tower, Valentina Pavlovna lay with her muzzle turned away from me, but I noticed that she kept her ears up and turned back a little. She was listening for my movements. Her cubs were watching me, but as their mother was near and she was quiet, they were unconcerned.

I spent about ten minutes at the base of the tower moving around and taking pictures. At one point, I walked slowly, pretending to be a bear, for about eighty feet (25 m) from the base of the tower. At that moment, Valentina Pavlovna decided she had had enough. She got up from the day bed, looked at me angrily, and started to approach. Her cubs joined her, and the three bears, with the angry female in the middle, walked toward me shoulder to shoulder sniffing the air. I saw what was happening and prepared myself to confront them. I put my camera away and picked up a heavy six-foot (2-m) stick. Then I took two steps toward them to show them that I was not going to back down.

The bears continued their slow approach. Valentina Pavlovna's face did not look promising. I stood like a bull with my legs wide, my head down a little in the direction of the team of bears, and my hands in front of me brandishing the stick. The bears stopped, sniffed, looked, and continued forward. Valentina Pavlovna continued to approach, making short investigative stops every three to four seconds. The last stop she made was forty feet (12 m) away from me. From that distance she started her first attack, not running yet but walking fast with her head down and forelegs stepping out wide. When she was about thirty feet (10 m) from me, I launched a counterattack. I took a couple of quick steps toward her, and when she was within reach, I struck the

ground in front of her with the stick. I also hissed at her. She stopped. Now she was more nervous, making "uphh . . . up-hh" sounds as she moved her head from side to side and gnashed her teeth. Her cubs were still at her side. They imitated her nervous noises and swung their heads from side to side as well.

I decided to take the initiative and attacked, taking four rapid steps forward and striking Valentina Pavlovna on the shoulder with the stick. As I did this, she rose up on her hindlegs to free her forepaws for a fight. Her head was up and her body was aimed slightly forward as if she were going to pounce. This was different from the way a polar bear stands up straight on its hind legs when it is simply looking for something it cannot see from the ground. She stretched out her forepaws to hit me, but my stick was long enough to keep her out of reach. She got back down on all fours, and I struck her again, this time on the cheek. She backed away a little, turning her head from the blow. Then she stopped her attack and went back to moving her head slightly from side to side while gnashing her teeth.

She remained in that position for a few seconds and then made her second attack. This time she kept her head down. Her cubs were still on either side of her. The three bears ran at me and stopped thirteen feet (4 m) away after I struck the ground with the stick right in front of Valentina Pavlovna's nose. Then I immediately picked up the stick and aimed the end of it at her face. (This is the way walruses defend

Valentina Pavlovna rose up before me on her hind legs to free her forepaws for a fight. Her head was up and her body was aimed forward as if she were going to pounce.

themselves against polar bears—by aiming their tusks at them). The bear stepped back and stopped twenty feet (7 m) from me. She did not look happy.

We confronted each other like this for about thirty seconds, and then she made her third attack. This time she was even more determined. She ran toward me with her head down and her cubs at her shoulder. I thought she was beautiful in her fury. I met her using the same walrus defense tactic, striking the ground in front of her nose and then aiming the stick at her face. She came to an abrupt halt six feet (2 m) from me. Again, we confronted each other for a few seconds before she slowly backed away. I did not budge. She retreated for fifteen feet or so (5 m) before she turned away from me and went off with her cubs following her. I could clearly see on her face that she was not satisfied with the results of our confrontation.

When interacting with her, I had acted automatically, not thinking about the possible outcome. After she retreated, I had plenty of time to reflect on what might have happened. The next day I had to force myself to walk to the end of the spit. I did not know whether Valentina Pavlovna would try to challenge me again. Much to my relief, she did not. After that interaction, she preferred to keep her distance, and I did the same.

In all my experience with polar bears, this was the only encounter that could have been really dangerous for me. The bear was highly motivated. She was angry and she wanted to see me off as if I were another bear. Had I not been able to manage the interaction, and had we actually come into physical contact with one another, things would not have gone well for me. Fortunately, I was able to anticipate her moves and intentions. It is important to note that I provoked the attack by moving around near her day bed. It is also important to note that even under such circumstances, it was possible to manage an interaction with an angry mature polar bear in a safe way using only behavioral means. This, I felt, was adequate proof that my theory about interacting with polar bears was valid.

This interaction was a really valuable experience for me. As I looked into Valentina Pavlovna's angry, beautiful face, I felt I was looking right into her soul. I know now what a bear sees when it is attacked by another bear. No wonder threatening displays are effective in seeing off opponents without need of physical contact—the face of an attacking polar bear is a truly fearsome sight.

Valentina Pavlovna was a high-ranking female. She was confident, even aggressive. On more than one occasion I observed her attacking and pushing away adult males. The day we fought she was not in a good mood. Perhaps she was hungry and that caused her to be more

Diving for food
On Wrangel Island, polar bears do not need to go far off shore to hunt seals, so rich are the hunting habitats in this part of the Arctic. This male bear was not feeding on seals or walruses, but was diving into a shallow lagoon to get to a beached gray whale. In advanced autumn, when the lagoon started to freeze over, the bears kept the hole in the ice open to reach the whale carcass that was lying just under the water. White seagulls waited close by, hoping for scraps.

In all my experience with polar bears, this was the only encounter that could have been really dangerous for me. The bear was angry and she wanted to see me off.

aggressive than usual. I could only guess. When I left the spit that day, I heard the barking of walruses in the dusk. They sounded excited as if they were going to haul out. The barking continued into the darkness as I reluctantly left.

The next morning, Valentina Pavlovna was on the spit with only one cub. As I made my way to my observation point, I noticed a bear lying in bloody snow on a day bed about halfway to the top of the spit. I did not approach the bear because wounded animals are often unpredictable. When the bear remained motionless for two more days, I realized it was dead, and I went to examine the carcass.

I caught my breath when I saw the animal. The two-year-old female lay stretched out on her belly sixty feet (20 m) from the water's edge as if she had died while trying to haul herself up the beach. There were five bloody holes in her body: two on the back of her head, two on her back, and one on the back of her left hind leg. My first thought was that she had been shot, but there were no ships in the area and I doubted she would have been able to swim far with two bullet holes in her head. Closer examination revealed the actual cause of death—walrus tusks.

I deeply regretted having missed this event. I could only guess at what had happened. Maybe Valentina Pavlovna was so hungry that she had attacked a group of walruses—which this year could have been composed mostly of males—and the cubs had been involved in the action. Or maybe the young cub had carelessly approached walruses on her own.

The incident brought home to me just how fragile life is in the Arctic. Protected by modern technology and well-equipped against the elements, we humans tend to forget this—until our equipment fails. We would do well to be mindful of our privileges at all times and to remember to respect the animals' right to life. After all, it is often people who pose the greatest threat to the animals' existence.

Now I had more answers to the puzzle about why polar bears are wary of walruses in the water. If the situation gets out of hand, either side may lose so each has to exercise care around the other. But this was not the most important thing that I learned. My observations taught me something that scientists have doubted for a long time—that polar bears do actively hunt walruses and use them as an essential source of food. This new knowledge is important for the long-term study of the life-cycles of walruses and polar bears as both seek to rebuild their populations and survive. From what I observed on Wrangel, it is clear that their predator-prey relationship affects the behavior and survival strategies of both species.

The incident brought home to me just how fragile life is in the Arctic. Protected by modern technology and well-equipped against the elements, we humans tend to forget this—until our equipment fails. We would do well to be mindful of our privileges at all times and to remember to respect the animals' right to life.

Conclusion

Persecution and Protection

Many people view the polar bear as an aggressive and dangerous beast that is a threat to people who live and work in its range. During my four-year study, I deliberately experienced over 500 direct interactions with polar bears. In only five cases was I attacked. In four of these cases, the attacks were for effect only and posed no serious danger to me. In two of these four, I could have taken refuge in a shelter had I needed to. In the other two, the attacks were abruptly halted when I stood my ground, and I did not need to engage the animal. In only one incident, with Valentina Pavlovna, was I in serious danger; however, I had provoked this confrontation, and the bear was not going to kill me but only push me away as she would have done any other bear. Even in that extreme case I was able to stop the bear by using only a long, heavy stick.

It is natural for a large predator that lives in a harsh environment such as the Arctic to investigate any strange creature it cannot identify from a distance. When a bear recognizes the creature is a human being, it will run away, but few people can stand a short distance from a polar bear without thinking that the bear is going to attack. Most people simply shoot the bear without waiting to see what will happen. Despite what my experience has shown about the nature of polar bears, I recognize that is not practical for most people to interact with them the way I do. It requires strong nerves as well as professional knowledge and training. There are things that can be done, however, to make encounters less risky—both for the human and for the bear.

"Dancing" bears, Cape Blossom

A group of four polar bears circle around each other at the perimeter of my observation camp, looking as if they are doing a folk dance. I lived alongside the polar bears of Wrangel and Herald Islands for four years and experienced more than 500 direct interactions with the bears. Despite the long-standing myths of man-killing polar bears, I found the bears to be inquisitive and largely peaceful toward me—good neighbors, in fact.

First of all, try to avoid surprise encounters by being aware of your surroundings. The sudden appearance of another creature at close quarters can cause defensive aggression even in a mouse. Remember that polar bears are inquisitive. To discourage them from hanging around your cabin or camp, do not leave food or garbage where they can get at it, and scare them off if they get in the habit of appearing at the door. Never feed them by hand and do not approach polar bears while they are feeding—a few of them may reasonably try to defend their meal. Take care not to put yourself between a mother and her cubs.

If you see a bear in the distance, do not try to attract its attention; however, if the bear sees you and starts to approach, never run away. Stand your ground and let the bear smell you. If you can, force yourself to take the initiative by moving aggressively toward the approaching bear, preferably when you are upwind of it. If you think you might meet bears, arm yourself with a long stick. It may help in an extreme situation. Remember, active actions are always the best for self-defense and for defending others.

Polar bear tracks, Wrangel Island
Tracks of polar bear families lead off the snow from Wrangel and onto the sea ice. Polar bears live in an environment threatened by ecological degradation and human hunting and encroachment. In the modern world, large predators are among the animals most threatened by humans. Polar bears have as much right as we do to be here.

Myths about polar bears have influenced public opinion. Gaps in scientific knowledge are filled by guesswork and fanciful suggestions.

⁓

Myths about polar bears have influenced public opinion since the first Arctic expeditions. Gaps in scientific knowledge are filled by guesswork and fanciful suggestions. Writers who include this misinformation in their published works contribute to the worldwide misunderstanding of the species and its behavior. If we carefully examine descriptions of the few reported incidents of a polar bear threatening a person's life in the Arctic, we find that all these incidents were provoked by people. The polar bears involved were often mothers forced to defend their cubs, or bears that were chased and cornered or that had been carelessly trained to lose their natural fear of humans by being fed by hand or by having food put out for them.

There are an incredible number of stories about polar bears terrorizing brave polar veterans, who had no choice but to "shoot the beast." I am amazed how similar and primitive these stories are. Ultimately, they are not about bears terrorizing humans, but about humans who fear this large white predator simply because it is there. The polar bear was never a threat to our survival in the Arctic. It is human beings who have persecuted polar bears in their native lands and pushed them to the brink of extinction.

⁓

The first colonists to arrive on Wrangel Island were four white men and an Inuit woman sent by Vilhjamur Stefansson in 1921. Environmental conditions that year were similar to the seasons I spent observing polar bears, with open sea around the island and many bears on the shore. The party landed on September 15, met their first polar bear on September 22, and shot it. As they needed food to eat and skins to earn a living, they shot every polar bear they met and left the carcasses on the tundra until snowfall, intending to collect them later by dog sled.

Later, however, they found the cached bear carcasses had been consumed by wildlife.

For two years the colonists on Wrangel struggled to survive, hunting anything that moved. Eventually, all four men died and countless numbers of polar bears paid with their lives for somebody's passion to experience risk and adventure in the High Arctic. In 1924, the Soviets displaced the illegal Canadian settlement from Wrangel, but for the polar bears it did not matter much under which flag they were persecuted.

A permanent Soviet settlement was established on Wrangel in 1926. Since that time, the exploitation of the island's wildlife had been steadily and rapidly expanding. The Soviets realized what Stefansson only dreamt of. They hunted and trapped and introduced reindeer herding to a land that had never known grazing animals. Later they built a military airstrip and a second settlement. Hunting polar bears remained a priority until 1956, when the Soviet government declared the bears to be protected throughout the Russian sector of the Arctic.

In his book, *Wrangel Island,* the second governor of the settlement on Wrangel, Aref Mineev, left a comprehensive description of polar bear hunts in the thirties. About seventy adult bears were killed every year. Bears were shot year round; however, only single animals could occasionally be killed in summer, and only about 10 percent of the harvest was taken in the autumn. Most bears were shot in the spring. The victims of this hunt were mothers with cubs.

About mid-March, when mother polar bears came out of their dens, hunters left the village to search for dens on the tundra. Usually, a hunter did not risk taking on a bear alone. As soon as a hunter located a den, he marked the entrance with a red flag or jacket on a stick to keep the female inside, and rushed back to the settlement for help. Sometimes the mother bear would leave the den despite the scarecrow, but many remained in their dens until the hunting team returned. Then hunters sent in dogs to force the bear to look out. They shot the bear when she lunged at the dogs. If a wounded bear tried to seek refuge in her den, the hunters would dig her out and shoot her at point-blank range. They would kill both mother and cubs, or they would take some of the cubs to the settlement to raise and kill later. There was one brave fellow who used to enter the dens by himself and shoot wounded females with a revolver.

Aref Mineev reported that in eight years of hunting polar bears this way not a single hunter was injured or killed by a polar bear. He also suggested that bears abandoned coastal denning habitats on the mainland when people settled in the vicinity and that they generally tried to avoid people. Despite intense hunting, however, Mineev reported that Wrangel continued to attract polar bears. Little wonder, since apart from Herald Island, there was no other solid ground in the Chukchi Sea. So polar bears continued to come, and their population in the region rapidly diminished.

There are numerous stories of polar bears terrorizing brave polar veterans, who had no choice but to "shoot the beast." Ultimately, they are not about bears terrorizing humans, but about humans who fear this large white predator simply because it is there.

The polar bears of Hudson Bay are the southernmost polar bear population in the world.

Playful bears, Cape Churchill
I was amazed by the playfulness of the Hudson Bay polar bears—even adult mature males were involved in play fighting. I never saw polar bears playing this much in the High Arctic

Polar Bears at Cape Churchill

Polar bears live in a remote and harsh environment, accessible to people only with difficulty. Due to this, one might expect polar bears to be better protected against humans than other large predators. This has not been the case, however. Polar bears appear to be one of the most vulnerable wildlife species to human impact. The invasion of the Arctic by Europeans has in a short time almost exterminated polar bears throughout extended portions of their original range.

To study polar bears to learn about their private lives, people would have to spend much of their lives in the Arctic among the bears, following them on their adventurous trails. How many people could do this? Not many, for sure. It is a privilege, but it is also a hard, risky, and ascetic way of life.

Does this mean that people interested in polar bears can watch them alive only in a zoo or on TV? Fortunately, this is not the case.

In autumn 1994, my good friend, Dan Guravich, invited me to visit the environmental education and polar bear viewing camp founded on Hudson Bay at Cape Churchill, Manitoba. Long before I had this chance to visit Cape Churchill, I knew about this special place.

The polar bears of Hudson Bay are the southernmost polar bear population in the world. They are also forced to spend more time on land than their relatives in the High Arctic. On Wrangel Island, polar bears are stranded on land once in every four or five years on average, and then only for brief periods. Only once in every ten or eleven years are the Wrangel bears stuck on land for long periods of thirty to forty-five days. The Hudson Bay bear population is forced to stay on land for about four months *every* year. This is an unusual and stressful situation for this marine predator.

After four seasons on Wrangel, I was anxious to see congregations of polar bears in a different region to compare impressions. So I accepted Dan's invitation with pleasure—although with a feeling of apprehension as well. For the first time since I had lived freely among polar bears, I now had to change my way of watching the bears, viewing them from the window of a tundra buggy. I was afraid that I would be disappointed with the research season. The lack of freedom to follow individual animals or search out particular situations is a serious limitation for research.

Despite these fears, observations on Hudson Bay became an essential contribution to my understanding of polar bear behavior. The environmental conditions at Hudson Bay provide unique opportunities for viewing polar bears without harassing them.

We watched some sixty polar bears near the Cape Churchill camp area in the fall of 1994. Polar bears of both sexes and all age groups visited the camp and socialized with each other. Tundra buggies, used as moving blinds, enabled researchers to follow and approach particular animals wherever they go: to the beach to eat kelp, to the bay's bank to make day beds in the soft snow blown over the willows, or even to follow—carefully and unobtrusively—a mother with her cubs to watch one of the most charming and private moments, the nursing of the cubs.

Based from the camp, people had a great opportunity to see polar bears in their natural world and, in particular, a lot of social interactions in variable combinations. One thing amazed me most of all: the incredible amount of play among the Hudson Bay polar bears. Even adult mature males were involved in play fighting. I never saw polar bears playing so much in the High Arctic. Polar bears of the Hudson Bay seemed to be more infantile compared to their relatives from the higher latitudes.

Dan Guravich should be congratulated for his polar bear viewing camp. His idea was to provide an alternative to the hunting of Hudson Bay polar bears, and his plan has been perfectly realized in cooperation with Len Smith, who built all of these unique facilities. During the fifteen years of its history, the camp on Cape Churchill has been developed into a well-organized, comfortable, and transportable Arctic field station for environmental education. Here people can share the privilege of touching Arctic nature and learning about the polar bear's natural life. This is a promising experience, which, together with good books and films about polar bears, may help to open human minds to a true understanding of the ice bear—and to think of its future.

One thing amazed me most of all: the incredible amount of play among the Hudson Bay polar bears. Even adult mature males were involved in play fighting.

The thirties were also a time of great exploration in the Arctic. Mineev explains: "From exploration ships, polar bears were shot for sport. Everybody who participated in an Arctic expedition wanted to be able to boast to his friends: 'I killed a polar bear!'" Before the killing of polar bears from ships was prohibited by the Soviet North-Passage Administration, Mineev says, "As soon as a bear was sighted, everybody who had a rifle collected at the bow to shoot the beast in a hail of bullets."

Mineev was the first to advocate the regulation of polar bear hunting on Wrangel Island. He did this because he was opposed to waste and over-harvesting of wildlife resources. In those days, even the most environmentally enlightened people did not care about the ethical aspects of people's attitudes toward wild animals. Europeans were consumers of wildlife, and no other approach to wild animals made sense to them.

In later years, development joined hunting to put pressure on the island's wildlife. Settlers constructed an airport, a military base, weather stations, and mining camps. As the number of settlers increased, the two settlements grew. In 1976, in response to pressure by Soviet ecologists, a nature reserve was established on both islands and resource exploitation was stopped. The polar bears had gotten their native land back; however, even then people did not leave them alone. The scientists began to arrive.

Sun over the snow, Wrangel Island
There is no question that Wrangel Island—as well as Cape Churchill in Canada and several other sites around the world—offers a unique place to study polar bears. The question is how intensively should we study them? Does our need to gather information excuse our impact on the animals? These are difficult yet essential questions.

There is no question that Wrangel Island is a unique place to study polar bears. The question is how intensively should we study them? Does our need to gather information excuse our impact on the animals? How do the biologists who work in the denning areas in the spring balance the vulnerability of mothers with small cubs against their need to gather data? How much thought is given to using methods that disturb the bears as little as possible?

Every March and April on Wrangel, when in former times hunters would load their dog sleds, now rangers and scientists load their snowmobiles. As the bears become active, so do the scientists. Every day of good weather, pairs of rangers drive over two areas with a high density of polar bear dens—the Dream-Head Mountains and Cape Warring. The snowmobiles make a lot of noise when anxious mothers are considering the best time to lead their cubs out. In the 1980s, these den-counting surveys were carried out on foot. Snowmobiles allow researchers to cover larger areas. It is also more fun to drive up mountains than to walk. Nearly every spring, young cubs are found separated from their mothers in areas of high driving activity.

While some researchers are busy finding dens on the ground, others fly over the area to spot dens from the air. This intense monitor-

Parade of bears, Cape Blossom
A mother bear with her two cubs patrols the beach watching for walruses. The polar bear population around the world is thought to have recovered since most hunting was banned. Native peoples in Alaska and Canada still hunt polar bears by quota; this may stimulate Native peoples in Siberia to claim similar rights in the future.

ing of the population pressures the bears from both the ground and the air. In addition, from 1990 through 1994, mother bears with cubs on Wrangel Island were pursued on and around their denning areas from huge helicopters to be tranquilized and banded with radio collars that allow the bears to be tracked by satellite. The tranquilizers do not harm the bear, and the information from the collar tells more about the bear's movements than individual researchers observing bears could ever hope to gather.

No doubt this research is the only way to learn about the polar bear population in the Chukchi Sea; however, here again we face the problem of priorities and ethics. How extensive should this kind of research be? What should be our first concern: the cost of the project and the comfort of the researchers or the rights of polar bears to be undisturbed in their denning habitats? In 1991, I helped capture bears, and in 1991–1992, I counted dens on the ground. Indeed, I was one of the initiators of these two programs; however, when we planned this research, we suggested conducting these surveys for a maximum of three seasons. The work is now routine for every season, and I now regret my role in instigating this annual disruption of the polar bears' lives on Wrangel.

Improperly managed tourism in the Russian Arctic is creating yet another problem for the bears. Unfortunately, tourists find mother bears with cubs irresistible. There is a risk that the reserve administra-

I was one of the initiators of programs to study the polar bear; however, when we planned this research, we suggested conducting these surveys for a maximum of three seasons. The work is now routine for every season, and I now regret my role in instigating this annual disruption of the polar bears' lives.

Sunset on the polar bear?
There are numerous stories of polar bears terrorizing brave polar veterans, who had no choice but to "shoot the beast." Ultimately, these stories are not about bears terrorizing humans, but about humans who fear this large white predator simply because it is there. It is human beings who have persecuted polar bears in their native lands and pushed them to the brink of extinction.

tion, suffering funding cuts, may see guided tours of den sites as a possible source of income. Sometimes even people who have the animals' best interest at heart do not consider that the animals might prefer not to be seen at all. Even if the animals appear to tolerate our intrusion, our presence may influence their population structures and patterns of distribution in ways that are hard to detect. Making them tolerant of humans may also make them vulnerable to humans who do not wish them well.

Wildlife conservation professionals work to protect wild animals; however, professional priorities may serve current management needs, which may not necessarily coincide with long-term wildlife welfare. Administrations and bureaucracies come and go. They are run by people who may make mistakes and whose decisions are often dictated by political expediency. Polar bears cannot defend themselves against the human technological invasion of the Arctic; it is up to us to do this for them. Public awareness is a powerful tool. Each of us, by actively opposing misguided management decisions, can personally promote the polar bear's cause.

⌒

The polar bear population around the world is thought to have recovered since hunting was banned. The Soviet Union made hunting polar bears illegal in 1956. In 1973, the five nations that share the Arctic region signed a treaty protecting polar bears. The signatories were

Canada, the United States, Denmark (for Greenland), Norway, and the Soviet Union. The treaty is a step forward but it does not mean that the species is out of danger as the treaty does not ban hunting completely. The Native peoples in Alaska and Canada hunt polar bears by quota, and this may stimulate Native peoples in Siberia to claim similar rights.

Before 1990, polar bear mortality caused by humans in the Russian Arctic was primarily attributable to so-called forced shooting of dangerous bears. The advent of a market economy in Russia has greatly increased illegal demand for polar bear skins and gall bladders, and international opportunities for black market trading has stimulated an interest in poaching. Federal law still prohibits the killing of polar bears in Russia, but these laws cannot be enforced. In addition, in the present economic crisis, people in the Russian Arctic are turning to polar bears for food, and some firms are lobbying the government to allow western trophy hunters, whose activities are severely restricted in their own countries, to trade hard currency for the dubious pleasure of plunging a bullet into a polar bear. (From my experience, the polar bear is such a calm and curious creature that there can be nothing exciting about hunting it. You have only to sit and wait, and a polar bear will approach you.) We also do not know how increased pollution will effect polar bears, nor do we know what global warming means for them. What is clear is that in our rapidly changing world, polar bears could easily be in trouble again.

In the modern world, large predators are among the animals most threatened by humans. They need large ranges and therefore suffer from habitat degradation more than many other wild animals. Many people think of large predators in negative terms. They see them as being aggressive and competitive. Despite all our technological achievements, we remain biological beings, and our view of the world is colored by irrational emotional responses that often have no basis in fact. This matters today more than ever because of the power we have to influence the world around us. Large predators are not in an enviable position when we manage the earth's resources to satisfy only human needs.

Polar bears have as much right as we do to be here. As increased industrialization inevitably pushes polar bears, and many other species, to the frontiers, their only hope for survival is that more people will realize that it is our joint responsibility to let wild animals live freely in their native habitats. If we do not, we will lose not only wonderful specimens of the animal kingdom, but also ourselves. In conserving large predators, we test our capability to save nature; in conserving the polar bear, we test our capability to save the Arctic.

It took a long time and much bloodshed to establish democracy in certain parts of the world; however, all sacrifices will be for nothing if we now fail to turn human powers of reason and creativity to new environmental ethics and create a new ecological democracy.

Polar bears have as much right as we do to be here. We must let wild animals live freely in their native habitats. If we do not, we will lose not only wonderful specimens of the animal kingdom, but also ourselves.

Organizations Working for Polar Bears

For those who are interested in the current status of polar bears and protection issues, I certainly recommend joining Polar Bears Alive, a nonprofit organization dedicated to the worldwide protection of the polar bear. The group's newsletter is outstanding, providing up-to-the-minute information on polar bears around the world as well as a library of books, calendars, and more.

> Polar Bears Alive
> P.O. Box 66142
> Baton Rouge, LA 70896–6142
> Telephone: 601–335–2444
> Fax: 601–332–9528

Recommend Reading

Polar Bears with text by Ian Stirling and photographs by Dan Guravich is the most extensive natural history of the white bears. This large, oversize book was published in 1988 by the University of Michigan Press at Ann Arbor. Stirling is a senior research scientist for the Canadian Wildlife Service and an adjunct professor of zoology at the University of Alberta, and his thorough, informative text offers a full course on polar bear biology. Guravich's photography chronicles much of the white bear's behavior and life, although primarily in North America.

Polar Bear with photographs by Dan Guravich and text by Downs Matthews is a fine introduction to the white bears. It was published in 1993 by Chronicle Books of San Francisco. This is a fine, popular book about polar bears, based primarily on the bears at Cape Churchill, Canada.

Polar Bear Cubs, again with photographs by Dan Guravich and text by Downs Matthews, is an excellent book for children. It was published by Simon and Schuster Books for Young Readers and was the winner of a *Parenting* magazine award.

A Naturalist's Guide to the Arctic by E. C. Pielou is a fine overview of the biology of the High Arctic, although it focuses primarily on North America. This book serves as both a travel book and field guide, covering everything from polar bears to Arctic flowers, ice formations to polar night. It was published in 1994 by the University of Chicago Press in Chicago.

The Adventure of Wrangel Island by Vilhjalmur Stefanson offers more history of Wrangel. Stefansson was a controversial Arctic explorer, and as he was writing in the early part of this century, he put forward a lot of information about the Arctic that has later been proved incorrect. Still, this book, published in 1925 by the MacMillan Company, describes the discovery of Wrangel and details the first colonists and their polar bear hunts.

Index

About the Author

Nikita Ovsyanikov
The author observing polar bears along the northern coast of Wrangel Island in autumn 1992. (Photo by Irina Menushina)

Nikita Gordeevitch Ovsyanikov lived with polar bears on Wrangel and Herald Islands in the High Arctic off the coast of Siberia for portions of each year since 1990. During that time, he did not carry a rifle or pistol, choosing to walk among the bears in order to "interact with them as one animal to another," as he writes.

Born in Vienna, Austria, he is a citizen of the Russian Federation. He holds a Ph.D. in Zoology from the Institute of Animal Evolutionary Morphology, Academy of Sciences of the USSR. He made his first zoological expedition to Wrangel Island in 1977 and conducted a ten-year research project on the behavioral ecology of the Arctic fox on the island.

Since 1990, Nikita has studied the polar bears on the island, living alone among the bears during most of his research. In 1994, he was named Senior Researcher of the Wrangel Island State Nature Reserve. By 1995, he rose to the position of Senior Research Scientist for the Pacific Institute of Geography, Academy of Sciences of Russia. He is also a specialist on wolves.

Nikita has been bitten by animals around the world, including numerous bites by Arctic foxes, one wolf bite, and a bite by a poisonous snake during his first desert expedition. He has never been injured by a polar bear in more than 500 encounters with the white bears.

To date, Nikita has spent fourteen seasons in the High Arctic on various research projects, including two full Arctic winters in the region. He has written over fifty scientific articles and several popular reports on Arctic wildlife and nature conservation. He also served as a scientific consultant and organizer for BBC TV Productions on Wrangel Island, including the documentaries *Realms of the Russian Bear* and *Trails of Life*.

He is passionately interested in problems of wildlife conservation in the former Soviet Union, and worked as an expert and advisor to both the previous leadership and the present Russian government for legislation on protection of wildlife.

Nikita enjoys traveling, canoeing, and downhill skiing. He believes he is the only person to downhill ski on Wrangel and Herald Islands—after the polar bears left in the spring for the ice, of course. The skiing on Herald was the most exciting of his life.

He is married to fellow scientist Irina Menushina and has one daughter. When not walking among the bears, he lives in Moscow.